Thank God

D1450866

Detour Before Midnight

Freedom Summer Workers: James Chaney,
Michael Schwerner, and Andrew Goodman
Made an Unscheduled Stop

To: Temple Beth Israel

Bernice Sims, LCSW

Bernice Sims

"History is, NOT WAS"

ISBN: 0989147703
ISBN-13: 9780989147705

Library of Congress Control Number: 2014904247
SimsBernice713, Mineola, NY

CONTENTS

INTRODUCTION

After the Mississippi Klan shot the three civil rights volunteers in 1964, their bodies were quickly loaded into their Ford station wagon and they were buried in Philadelphia, Mississippi. A leader in this lynch mob told the group of conspirators, "Well, boys, you've done a good job. You've struck a blow for the white man. Mississippi can be proud of you. You've let those agitating outsiders know where this state stands. Now go home and forget it." *Detour* recalls the memories of one who could not forget: a volunteer who had just spent time with them a few hours before their abduction. James Chaney, Michael Schwerner, and Andrew Goodman made an unscheduled stop at her home. *Detour* examines this volunteer's seasoning, which prepared her for a life bound to intersect with those of the three martyrs before Freedom Summer. She was the butterfly waiting for the net, not destined to take flight. She was the bee waiting to make the honey in spite of the foretold sting. You will discover that she was a willing recruit called to fight in a battle that originated in her soul and can only be understood as something larger than reasonable comprehension. The embryo had been implanted by her struggles and seasoning. This recollection details this colleague's seasoning, which created the perfect recipe for partnership with Mickey, James, and Andy. They were her neighbors, friends, and colleagues, with whom she had worked side by side as a volunteer with CORE/COFO in Mississippi. Her memoirs string together her life as she negotiated living in the Jim Crow South before she and James Chaney (Martyr) were recruited by Martyr Michael Schwerner to work in the movement.

The civil rights movement was traumatized by the tragedy of President John F. Kennedy's assassination. However, sympathy associated with his death propelled the passage of the 1964 Civil Rights Act signed by President

Johnson. Soon after the movement was recovering from the setback, several murders took place, including those of three civil rights volunteers: James Chaney, a black Mississippian, Michael Schwerner and Andrew Goodman, white New Yorkers. *Detour* recalls how the three civil rights workers went off their schedule to visit a family in Meridian, Mississippi, just thirty five miles from Philadelphia, where they were falsely arrested, detained, and released into the hands of the Mississippi KKK. They spent some of their last few precious hours in the home of this volunteer on June 21, 1964. Why did they go off schedule? What role did this volunteer play in their lives during Freedom Summer?

This is an untold story that reflects upon that historic and heinous crime committed during the Mississippi summer movement.

There have been much written about the abduction and murder of the three civil rights workers by the Mississippi KKK on June 21, 1964. There have been numerous stories in the news, as well as movies and TV docudramas, which have depicted this heinous crime that took place at the height of Freedom Summer. Three young martyrs were found in an earthen grave in Philadelphia, Mississippi, forty-four days after their abduction. *All three were shot before midnight.* Over the years, this volunteer has avoided many invitations to attend annual memorials commemorating their deaths, as part of her grief process. In 2005, however, she accepted her first invitation to speak at the forty-first commemorative anniversary, where she spoke publicly for the first time about the last time that she saw the trio. It was the same year that the alleged orchestrator of the mob conspiracy was finally brought to trial. Edgar Ray Killin was finally convicted in 2005. That year represented several firsts for the author. She saw the widow of Michael Schwerner and the brother of James Chaney for the first time in over forty-one years. It was that same year that she visited Jackson, Mississippi, and saw the memorial for Medgar Evers. The civil rights leader and field secretary for the Mississippi NAACP was gunned down in his driveway on June 12, 1963. She had been in his home a few days before that murder took place. She had been a guest there after attending a rally at his church listening to the then national director of the NAACP foretelling the planned Freedom Summer Campaign. She was a youth with the NAACP and had been involved in protest marches and antidiscrimination activities during the sixties.

She ate lunch in Medgar Evers's home a few feet away from where he was assassinated weeks later.

The Civil Rights Movement and Freedom Summer were characterized by demonstrations, freedom rides, and sit-ins, initiated by African-American students in 1960 and 1961. By 1962, freedom was in the air. Student-led sit-ins spread throughout the South. The Congress of Racial Equality (CORE) initiated the "freedom rides" to end discrimination on interstate public transportation.

Both sit-ins and freedom rides had been lead stories on national TV news. Mississippi was on fire. In the 1960s, the Southern Christian Leadership Conference (SCLC) led marches and mass demonstrations challenging segregation head-on in the cities across the South. In the early 1960s, the SCLC initiated a citizenship education program to prepare black voters to vote. The NAACP was filing briefs against various forms of legal segregation in the South, and its chapters there were small centers of resistance to Jim Crow.

By the early 1960s, a consensus in the Southern movement had emerged: organizing around the right to vote was the key to black freedom. Again and again, black citizens sought the right to register to vote only to be denied by county clerks and other registrars of voters. Community centers were bombed. At the polls, various forms of intimidation could take place ie. a potential black voter could be challenged by a large jar of jellybeans on the desk of the examiner. "Guess how many jellybeans are in this jar as a prerequisite to vote,. An official at city hall would pick out random selected sections of the state constitution, and ask him to interpret it. A task that was impossible for many legal scholars. Many times black citizens would be slipped a card from someone lurking the shadows. They would slip a card near potential black voters when they went to the court houses to try to vote. The card, complete with two big red eyes with these printed words: "The eyes of the Klan's are upon you. You have been identified by the white knights of the Ku Klux Klan."

"Reach Out and Touch Somebody's Hand, Make This World a Better Place if You Can" (Diana Ross)

In 1962 a small group of students left their studies and began full-time work as community organizers in the black belt counties of the Deep South.

The main focus of the small group of community organizers was upon registering African Americans to vote. They included the Student Nonviolence Coordinating Committee (SNCC), Mississippi Freedom Democratic Party (MFDP), Congress of Racial Equality (CORE), Council of Federated Organizations (COFO), and other initiatives for justice in the South.

The plan of this challenge was to bring black and white students as summer volunteers to work along with local groups. The course of Freedom Summer changed Mississippi forever. CORE was initiated under the umbrella of pacifism and applied nonviolent direct action toward racial discrimination. Members' actions often led to beatings, arrests, and murder.

This book will serve as an overall guide and provide an additional vehicle to educate students and others about the Veterans of the Mississippi Freedom Summer Movement, and the sacrifices that they made. The book is written from a personal rectrospectius and eyewitness account.

It can serve as a guidebook for our conscience. Our right to vote is being threatened today and can easily be lost through neo–Jim Crow language. Today's voter suppression laws may not look the same on the books as they were in the 1960s; however, the residual effects still ring true.

New laws and regulations are surfacing every day. People today, young and old, are unaware of the many battles fought for these freedoms. This page of history is missing from schoolbooks. Some school districts have selected to rewrite African slave history, and saying that the "Middle Passage" did not exist, in an attempt to marginalize the inhumanity of slavery.

They were partners in the fight for freedom in Jim Crow Mississippi via CORE (Congress of Racial Equality)and COFO (Coordinated Federation of Organizations). There existed a partnership among the three workers and this colleague in 1964 at the height of the Freedom Summer Movement. This recollection reveals how she met the trio, and how they became partners. They were partners in the fight for freedom in Jim Crow Mississippi via CORE (Congress of Racial Equality)and COFO (Coordinated Federation of Organizations).

Detour provides some insight into the three workers and what bonded them together. They found in her a fighting partner who had never accepted Jim Crow in spite of being surrounded by it all of her life. She was among a group of teens just waiting for directions to a place that could be understood only in light of a moment whose time had just come. She found herself called for a battle that could only be understood as something larger than reasonable comprehension. She was connected to the movement before it came to her hometown. The embryo had been implanted by her struggles and seasoning, partly by being born a girl overshadowed by four brothers. She was the implanted struggling embryo just waiting to take a breath and blow into a soul that was ready for birth. She revisited some of the turbulent years of the early 1960s that shaped many of us and challenges us not to forget: the 1963 assassinations of Medgar Evers and President John F. Kennedy and the horrendous murders of four little girls killed by a bomb blast in their church basement as they waited for church in Birmingham, Alabama, among others. In the year 2014, we will commemorate the fiftieth Anniversary of the deaths of Freedom Fighters James Chaney, Andrew Goodman, and Michael Schwerner, who were abducted and killed by the Mississippi Ku Klux Klan. The election of our first black president has renewed interest in the 1960s movement.

This year, more than ever, has rekindled memories of that most heinous crime committed on the battleground for voter registration.

The three martyrs didn't go directly to bloody Neshoba County to meet their fate. They made an unscheduled stop to see a friend and colleague. This memoir provides some insight into this unscheduled stop. It is an intimate and personal portrayal of a family they had become close to during Freedom Summer.

For almost three years, she was among a group of activist teenagers in Meridian being groomed for the Mississippi challenge of 1964. These groups of teens were unaware initially that they had been strategically selected and positioned to be active partners in the fight for equality in Mississippi.

The fact that these efforts were in place without the full knowledge of these teens meant that they entered into a silent partnership. In some published writings, they have been referred to as "the Kids." A handpicked selection of kids was asked to submerge themselves into the early waters to test the civil rights movement in Meridian, Mississippi, and neighboring rural communities.

This recollection reveals how she met the trio of freedom fighters and how they became partners. The story describes how she negotiated education, relationships with family, church, political and emotional life in order to meet the challenge that fostered the relationship between Chaney, Schwerner, and Goodman.

This work is a memoir, which reflects the author's present recollections of her experiences over a period of years.

These recollections focus upon the birthplace of James Chaney and the significance of Meridian, Mississippi, in the whole scheme of the civil rights movement. It is the home of the sheriff who identified and maintained surveillance and kept the pulse on the movement.

This sheriff provided logistical information to other Klan members to carry out the plans of abducting the three and carrying out their murders, which were to prevent black voting advancement and were meant to stifle equality and keep liberty at bay or from taking place.

Meridian was one of the epicenters of all civil rights and Freedom Summer activities taking place in 1964. Meridian was the birthplace of James Chaney and the assigned workplace of his colleagues: Michael Schwerner and Andrew Goodman. This Southern town is again being thrown into the spotlight in the year 2014, with the fiftieth anniversary remembrance of their murder. In Meridian and other locations, people will be commemorating and honoring the three fallen civil rights martyrs with the dedication of the first civil rights museum in Meridian. Plans are underway to establish a community center to service the local youth using the 1964 model, which provided educational, cultural, creative, and social enrichment for children and families.

It is a story that has never been told about the last hours of the three martyrs' lives. This memoir will serve as a vehicle to encourage others confronted by tragedy to move forward. Her story represents the completion of the grief process. The author shares with her readers answers to many lingering questions about the trio's state of mind on that awful day.

Many take the right to vote for granted and forget that lives were lost for such a precious right. Today, those rights are again being threatened.

In the 1960s, black citizens sought the right to register to vote only to be denied by county clerks and other registrars of voters. Designated locations, including churches and community centers, were bombed. Underhanded intimidation took place at the polls.

The 1965 Voting Rights Act that gave one the right to vote without harassment at the polling places had a shelf life. It was not a permanent law. In addition to that procedural oversight, new laws have passed around the country that restrict the pool of eligible voters and make it harder for Americans to cast a ballot, representing a step backward in a decades-long struggle to end discrimination in this country. We don't want America to turn back the clock on the fundamental right to vote. The Supreme Court (SCOTUS), which in the summer of 2013, gutted part 4 regarding preclearance, did not make it any easier. Preclearance is related to providing protection at the polls. Several states took immediate actions when SCOTUS eliminated this status. Voter suppression laws raised their ugly heads. In over thirty-four states, new laws to suppress voting emerged, which could have affected nearly five million voters in the 2012 election. There is nothing more fundamental to our democracy than the right to vote.

Legislative action sponsored by the current dominant political party–led state legislatures is making it harder for voters to cast ballots.

This book will serve as an overall guide and provide an additional vehicle to educate students and others about the participation of youthful veterans of the Mississippi Freedom Summer movement and the sacrifices they made and courage they demonstrated for causes loftier than they fully comprehended.

Today's voter suppression laws may not look the same on the books as they did in the 1960s; however, the residual effects still ring true. The biting dogs, billy clubs, poll taxes, and water hoses have been replaced with long lines at the polling places; shorter days to vote; and voter ID laws seasoned with locations inconvenient for the poor and elderly, minorities, and students. We have been able to see the eradication of an important cultural tradition in the black church on Sundays. "Taking the souls to the polls" after attending church services. The elimination of Sunday voting has resulted in having shorter days, and longer lines at the polls.

New laws and regulations are surfacing every day. New words and terms are being used to minimize the ugliness of slavery and Jim Crow. Young people read about Jim Crow laws regarding black and white water fountains and think that it can't happen today and it is preposterous thinking. There are many who are puzzled by recent acts to humiliate, minimize, and dehumanize people of color with signs of hate and disrespect on college campuses, governemnt buildings, and the White House Lawns.

These rights securing a rightful place at the polling booth were fought for in a war that left many victims with visible and invisible scars. Some are associated with the violence and intimidation experienced at the hands of the white supremacists. Other invisible scars are from survivor's guilt, pain, and internal suffering. The fights, the struggles, and the losses endured during the sixties were too arduous and painful to have to repeat. The 1965 Voting Rights Act gave one the right to vote without having to be harassed at polling places. Unfortunately, it was not intended to last forever.

*"There still exists the possibility that one can make a difference. An individual can assist and effect change."***(Author)**

*"For those who have been historically disenfranchised and denied, who struggled, fought, and won the right to vote, voting is sacred."***(Author)**

"History is not was, but is" (Ken Burn)

Upon the fifty-year anniversary on June 21, 2014, of their deaths, perhaps we can answer the questions: Did they die in vain? Were they victims, or is there victory? We can celebrate their lives with a newfound activism giving testimony to their heroism. They were idealists, committed and willing to put their lives on the line to fight for what they believed in, to right the wrongs of past injustices.

We still need that kind of youthful passion and energy to keep the world alert because what was fought for and won can be easily taken or stolen. We must remain vigilant, and we cannot rely upon past accomplishments.

In Florida, the sitting governor passed a House Bill 1355, which requires voter registration groups to preregister with the state before engaging in any voter registration activity. All registration material must be delivered within forty-eight hours of voter signatures. Monthly reports must be filed with state restrictions on early/absentee ballots. Executive action making it harder to restore voting rights taken in restriction on a voter's registration passed. All was done in an effort to give their party an unfair advantage. Sunday voting restrictions before elections and voter identification will affect minorities, the elderly, and students. The new voter suppression initiatives of today will offer the same results as the Jim Crows laws of the 1960s: the absence of your voice and denial of your right to participate in the democratic process.

How This Book Should Be Read

In the first three chapters, the author reflects upon how her life seasoning prepared her for a life bound to intersect with those of Freedom Summer volunteers. In the following three chapters (4, 5, and 6), she reflects upon her activism in NAACP, *the trio's state of mind before their abduction,* Freedom Summer, and with the Mississippi Freedom Democratic Party, which was the nexus of the Mississippi Summer movement. In chapters 7, 8, and 9, she reflects upon the crime, coping with their loss, the justice system's resolution, and many unresolved questions remaining about the case. In chapter 10 and the epilogue, the author takes the opportunity to offer some personal reflections and reexamine the social and political climate in 1964 in comparison to our current climate.

These recollections detail this colleague's seasoning, which created the perfect recipe for partnership with Mickey, James, and Andy, her neighbors, friends, and colleagues with whom she had worked side by side. This is another story that almost got buried alongside them in their earthen grave.

CHAPTER ONE

Seasoning: Family Foundation

"Keep On Pushing" Curtis Mayfield and The Impressions"

Seeking equality and justice may have been in my DNA. My enthusiasm can probably be traced to three things: birth order, patriotism or political interest, and religious upbringing. It could have been the result of birth order, having been surrounded by four male siblings. My female siblings were either too old or too young to be my immediate companions. My playmates by default were my brothers and their male friends. The order of my birth possibly started me out negotiating for my rightful place in this male-dominated home environment. My interest in social justice probably had something to do with being thrown in the middle, the seventh of thirteen children. I was just fighting every day for some form of justice for myself. It was an odd place to be, raised mainly around boys, while at the same time; I enjoyed the vicissitudes of being the female. We would fight often, however, and being a female didn't get me much slack. Whenever our fight or bout reached my mother, we'd get punished. We all had to supply our own switches, which stung our legs. My mother would offer her assistance to find a larger switch if we presented her with the smallest twig from the tree branch. If we were still angry at each other after our bouts, she used another tactic to deal with us, which was probably worse than her first punishment: Upon completion of our heavyweight bouts, she would make us hug onto each other. I sometimes volunteered for an extra whipping rather than hold onto my "enemy brother." She would supervise a stand-up hugging. We had to hold onto each other without letting go until she felt that our venom had subsided. We'd have to hold onto to each other for what seemed like hours, focusing upon the wall, a picture, anything but each other. When we were able to look our "enemy" in the eye, we would laugh uncontrollably. Mother would be monitoring all of the hugging with her switch. Our weekly fighting bouts almost disappeared. I don't know what I hated more: the whippings or being forced to embrace my enemy in the aftermath of a battle. I didn't fight with my brother David often, and I think that it was because he seemed to have embraced me as a sibling playmate rather than a rival.

The Embryonic Seed: Racial Awareness

*"Amazing Grace: I once was lost, but now, I'm found,
was blind but now I see"*

We lived in the rural area until I reached age five. I suppose that we had been somewhat isolated in a small rural community that we referred to as Nelly burg. As a youngster, it seemed several miles away from "the city." I later learned that it was only about 5 miles from Meridian. Our next-door neighbors were a white family whom we referred to as "the Sullivan's." They had four children, and all of the age-appropriate children played together until sundown beckoned us to go inside on those long fun-filled summer days. My mother and "Miss Sullivan" exchanged recipes, did laundry together and offered childbearing assistance to each other. My dad and Mr. Sullivan planted crops and raised livestock.

The relationship between the two families may have appeared equal until the day that the Natchez cousin paid them a visit. David and I was Pat's playmate. We straddled his birthday; he was a year older than me and a year younger than David. This visiting cousin played the typical games with us throughout the countryside until the rain started. My brother decided to go into the house for some food and respite. I continued to play with my white male playmate and his cousin. We went into the barn where we could always find respite from the weather. In this barn, we had a hayloft, and we stored corn and cotton. It was warm, the cotton was soft and provided shelter from the rain, and we could go on for hours playing the typical childish games of our youth. We started a competitive game throwing sticks that we had gathered. Who could chunk the farthest? After it became apparent that I had the winning arm, and won every time, Natchez cousin got mad because I fairly won the stick-throwing contest. Everyone knew that I had a good right arm. He started name-calling, and he introduced me to the word *Nigger*. I instinctively knew that the word existed and felt it was meant to demean and insult. But this was the first time that I had heard a white person call me by that name. He didn't take well to being a loser, and he began to hit me with his hands. I fought back hard as my friend, Pat watched in disbelief, seeming confused about whom to side with. Things were getting pretty intense; I was now wondering what was keeping my brother. David eventually reappeared in the barn to rescue me, just in time. He came in and began to slug the Natchez cousin, and a fight ensued and proceeded all over the barn. The Natchez cousin seemed to have obtained more bruises to that porcelain skin from a combination of stickle straw and sticks. I was confused, hurt, and disappointed, especially by the no action of my longtime friend, Pat. He seemed caught between a vice, two worlds. I became acutely aware that somehow this incident would be associated with a permanent change in our childhood on this day. I instinctively knew that a sense of innocence had been lost. What would now happen to all the good times of the past? It was changed, and I found it disturbing. From that day forth, I never really enjoyed the companionship of my innocent white playmate, and I hated his cousin from Natchez who spoiled everything in one day. I also became keenly aware of the racial divides when I told my father about the fighting that had taken place in the barn. He became so angry and proceeded to handle that incident like he was accustomed. Whenever we fought, everyone received corporal punishment.

We all got a whipping: Pat, the cousin, my brother, and me for fighting. I think that my brother got extra for abandoning me in the barn. Punishing offenders (all children) when there has been fighting was a normal ritual in our household. The Natchez cousin and Pat, however, showed more signs of their punishment that I noted were different than ours. There were so many more visible bruises and scratches on Pat and the Natchez cousin from the switching inflicted by my father. Both of my white playmates were still under my mother's care, because the Sullivan's were away on a day trip. My mother was upset with my father for using corporal punishment and taking the law into his own hands. After the punishment, my mother was busily applying ointments and salves to provide comfort to us from the results of dad's whip-pings. We were hopeful that the salve could remove some lasting scars. There appeared to be nothing strong enough to remove the scars and black and blue marks from Pat & Natchez cousin. I think that I hated them for not having skin like ours. *So translucence and tender,* I thought. I could hear my mother complaining about the possible repercussions and wrath from the Sullivan's and the possibility of police involvement. There was a sense of hush and fear pervading our home all day as we awaited the return of the Sullivan's. We just knew that my dad was in a unique position (second-class citizenry) that would somehow change the relationship between the families forever.

It seems that it wasn't thought about very much until this moment in time. Pat had always loved my mom's hotcakes. I believe that she cooked a mountain of hotcakes that day. I remember seeing Pat and his cousin eat hotcakes with syrup all day long. There was a silent and pervasive fear that penetrated the fabric of everything as we waited for the Sullivan's to return. I heard my parents' tense discussions and anticipation about of all the pos-sible repercussions of my dad whipping this white child. This was in the early 1950s after all. That Natchez Mississippi child just seemed to have so many black-and-blue marks that would probably remain forever. We had considered other possibilities—e.g., the cousin was picking blackberries and received scratches from briar patches, fell off an old horse, or contacted poi-son ivy. I had begun to feel guilty and think that everything was my fault because I was the one who told my parents about the incident. When the Sullivan's finally arrived home, my mom took the high road by telling her friend the truth about why my father got so angry, and included the cousin from Natchez for punishment.

I could hear my daddy saying he didn't care what the consequences were. He felt that he had to demonstrate protection for his baby girl. It ap-peared that Pat and his cousin were remorseful and cognizant that they were wrong, and took some responsibility. They were also rather frightened over this unique anger that they witnessed from the usual mild-mannered *Uncle Tommie, my dad.* The Sullivan's offered understanding and reassurance that they understood my daddy's anger. The relationship between Pat and me was never the same again. Our play was much more supervised, and we never saw the Natchez cousin return. If he visited Pat, we never knew about it. He never came to our house.

That particular incident on that day placed an indelible mark that could not be removed. My eyes were now opened with a keen awareness of race relations in my world. We subsequently moved to the city of Meridian, and all of my relationships were now black. In the city, our relationships with whites were more clearly defined. No more confusing relationships with the white Sullivan family, whom we had thought of as friends in our little isolated environment in the country. We didn't see them very much, so we didn't have to explain to anyone that we were friendly with a white family. We did continue to receive visits from members of the Sullivan family. Their two older sons could not resist the non-reciprocated affection of our "pretty sister." They used to fight over which one would marry her first. Both brothers vied for my sister Lillie's affection and continued to carry a torch for her years after our leaving the country. Whenever we were advised of their impending visit to our new home, we would hide her in the closet and protest her absence from the home. We didn't have to explain our past relationship with our new found Negro friends and associates in the city. We just allowed them to think that our relationship with this white family was associated with work. We never really felt obligated to explain to our black neighbors about the Sullivan's. After all, how could they understand that we had enjoyed this rare relationship with a white family in rural Mississippi?

Brothers' Boot Camp

"Ain't No Mountain High Enough" (Diana Ross)

My older sister's training was relegated to household duties within the home. My brothers knew that my mother was a little anxious about me being surrounded by four brothers. They seemed to take special pleasure in "toughening me up" as soon as I was able to endure their training. They took great care in preparing me so that I could survive in this mean, cruel world while in rural Mississippi. It appears that I adapted pretty well to the training and challenges that they put before me.

They taught me to fight like a boy, climb trees, and "skin the cat" (climb halfway up a tree and select a limb to do a summersault suspended in mid-air, and make a complete rotation by coming through my legs and arms for balance). The challenge was to support yourself by your upper body while suspended several feet above the ground without the protection of a net or mattress. They taught me to dig for earthworms, bait the hook, and accompany them on fishing trips. I'd race them and their friends up and down the hills, beating them up all along the way, jumping over barbed-wired fences in my specially fashioned pants, which I constructed by pulling my dresses between my legs and securing them with a wide belt at the waist. In my special tucked-in dresses, I did insist upon on remaining ladylike under my rigorous brother boot camp complete with pink ribbons in my hair. I eventually mastered, though with much trepidation, how to wring the neck of a live chicken in time for dinner. We all learned to plant and harvest vegetables, hoe and chop cotton, and milk the cow. Among my most challenging feats was milking our uncooperative cow, Bessie.

I ate the rosin from pine trees (that is the sticky, gummy, beige-looking substance that oozed from the pine tree). You could not get us to believe that it was not the base in which they made chewing gum. We ate wild berries, fruits, and nuts from trees, which we'd shaken down. We loved to sun bake crab apples from trees that we had personally shaken down. They tasted best when we sun baked these small apples for a few hours. We'd wash, peel, and thinly slice these sour apples and sprinkle them with salt. The thought of those sun baked crab apples stimulates my salivary glands just thinking about them. We jumped over streams, milked cows, and ate wild grapes and berries from trees, vines, and bushes. I shook the limbs of fruit trees until they hit the ground in ample amounts to take home a mess for pie making.

These were among some of my outdoor lessons taught by my male siblings. My mother was a staunch advocate of equal rights among the sexes; however, she had initially become concerned that my male siblings would overshadow or hurt me. Both male and female siblings were taught to do housework, hunt, fish, farm, plant and harvest fruits and vegetables, cook, sew, do laundry, draw water from the well, and sow, chop, and pick cotton. I usually kept my hair in place with ribbons and bows. I made my own durable comfort wear by converting dresses into Hammer-like pants held together by a large belt with a buckle, which allowed me to shadow them around, jumping over fences and watering holes and tributaries and combating neighbors who were chasing us in hot pursuit.

I was in hog heaven with my male siblings. I belonged to this unique male club/gang until I reached the age of thirteen. It was around this time that I began to experience alienation and rejection from my brothers. After all of the years of acceptance and bonding, they began to tell me that I could not hang out with them any more. I became keenly aware of this whenever their male friends were about. These same friends that I had endorsed and accepted as my pals only a few years earlier. They began to tell me that I could no longer hang out with them and their friends. It was a harsh reality that dealt a horrific blow to my 13 year old female comprehension. It took me years to recognize that their rejection was an act of love to protect their now budding adolescent sister. At the time, it was blow, because I didn't like being excluded. My mother also feared for my safety and vulnerability. As soon as I was old enough, my brothers had taught me to fight like a boy with my fists as opposed to swinging arms wildly at the wind like most girls fought at that time. They taught me how to box. This was supplemented by watching weekly boxing matches on TV every Friday night with my dad. My father and I watched often before the sport was removed from TV. I recall that the band followed the death of a boxer that occurred over the small screen. Friday-night boxing became a regular ritual for my dad and me. It was our quality time together. I don't know what I enjoyed most, seeing this usually mild-mannered diminutive man turn into the mighty hulk with expressions and gestures to match as he sanctioned the moves and motivation of the boxers as they exploded in exercising their killer instincts. Oh, what a joy it was to be with Dad as he demonstrated his approval. As I look back, I realize he was probably exercising the only release from the frustration of racism he had to endure daily. It didn't take long for my mother's anxieties to shift to more concern about what I was capable of doing to my brothers. My brothers today can show me battle scars that were supposed to have been inflicted by me on their heads, arms, or hands. My brothers indulged and supported my gutsy fearlessness and strength. My mother began to wonder what they had created. They had taken on the responsibility with pride to train me to be as tough as they were in order to ease some of Mother's anxieties. After a while, my mother began to worry about the boys, because I started to beat them up with whatever I could get my hands on in the southern countryside. I was very resourceful at chunking rocks, and using my little tight fists. There would be no peace if they bothered me unfairly. I had a long memory and lots of patience. If one of my male companions *"messed"* with me at the wrong time, they may get hit by one of my little hard fist. After awhile, my mother stopped worrying about me growing up with boys. The family crowns me with a new label: "devilish" among other names. I can recall being referred to by that name to describe many of my activities. "I heard it a lot." Now, you know that girl is devilish, so don't mess with her". Some were not so convinced to leave me along. They somehow wanted to challenge me to see what I was made of. I was quite self-sufficient, independent, and enjoyed my privacy.

COUSIN EDDIE:

I had a male cousin one year younger, who decided to test my tolerance one day at the wrong time. He began to call me names and launch other insults in my directions, which I could ignore because I was consecrating on an art project. I was creating a sand masterpiece using the ground as my canvass. He decided that he would come over to my space, and destroy my artistic expression. Well, this was the straw that broke the camel's back. I picked up a rock, and threw it at him, which landed on his forehead. I watched in amazement how this act caused a baking powder biscuit effect. I had never seen a knot rise like that on a person's head. I became frightened because I wondered how big it was going to get before it stopped growing. I remember repeating: "they told you to leave me alone, "they said that I was devilish" was my continuance mantra. All I know is that I was transfixed by what seemed like a forever growing knot on my cousin's forehead. As you may have guessed, he never challenged me again, and I learned the power of my rock throwing. Although I was about 5 years old, it was scary lesson that resonate today.

"RESOURCEFULNESS IN THE COUNTRY:

We just loved to get caught playing outside in a rainstorm. My brothers and I had constructed several cave-like shelters along our traveled routes throughout the countryside. We'd collect branches from tree limbs, rocks, strong leaves and plants to create these shelters to protect us from heavy rain. In the event that we were caught away from home when the hard rain would come, we'd always have our refuge. We continued to add volume to these cave like structures every time we went outside. We would layer and weave twigs, limbs, etc. in ways that would prevent rain leakage. Our structures became so thick with twigs and leaves that we rarely ever felt the rain come through. These makeshift shelters provided safety, and kept us dry as we waited out a rainstorm. We would tell ghost stories and tales of woe to entertain and try to our scare each other. The thundering and lightning never bothered us too much. This was largely due to my mom's astute way of combining child-drearing with our religious faith. She told us that the sound of loud thunder was God's way of speaking to us. She assured us that if we listened carefully enough, we could hear what God was saying. Each one of us sworn that we knew exactly what "He" was saying. These exercises challenged us to remain quiet, and practice good listening skills. Each one of us had a difference version of what we knew to be true of God's actual words.

Religion:

I am sure my religious upbringing played a major part in developing **my** attitude about racism, which could not be reconciled with my spiritual upbringing. I was taught that there was no one greater than God, the Supreme Being. He loved the world so much that he allowed his only son to come into this world and die for our sins. He became the sacrifices for all of our wrongs. There were also so many symbolisms that I could observe in our world that demonstrated that we valued God. Our money is closely aligned with our government belief system: On our money, we can see: In God we Trust. On the dollar bill and coins, God was always there. "In God we trust "stand. In school, every day, we pledged allegiance to the flag and our country as one nation, under God indivisible with liberty and justice for all. I brought into those concepts, hook line, and sinker. I begun to wonder how could my good all-powerful, omnipotent respected God makes one race superior to another? He created us all equally. So it was a no brainier for me. The superiority of any race over another in this Our God's Country was a concept that I could never ascribe too. That would be like calling God a Liar. In school, we were charged many scriptures especially psalms to take to memorizations. Exclusions (Jim Crow laws), along with so many of every day racism that we were forced to endure fueled my fire for justice and equality. It was also at this age that I became aware of social work advocacy. I had begun to think of racism as a form of mental illness.

My mother and father kept us in Sunday school and church every Sunday and sometimes during the week, especially if there was a revival going on or a convention-taking place. She and my father imparted good moral lessons to us all the time. We know the Ten Commandments, the Beatitudes; the Lord's Prayer, and many psalms and verses from the Bible because they quoted from them all the time. We had them, the church, the school, and neighbors, family, and friends to reinforce the values of living a clean life. She believed in God and the power of prayer. She would always say, "Don't forget to pray." She reminded us all the time that if we wanted something badly enough to first, "seek ye first, the kingdom of God", and He will grant to you your heart's desires".

"Signed, Sealed, Delivered" (Stevie Wonder)

The Mourning Bench

Our family went on many outings together, including church, the fair, and fishing trips. Most were associated with our church functions.

Attending church was an important part of our lives. Attending church on Sunday was an event that usually covered the entire day. This was the lifestyle of most southern colored people at that time—Sunday school, regular church services, Bible Training Union (BTU), and Sunday evening services. You were there for the whole day usually. Revival week was a big deal in the Southern Baptist scheme of things. They only came about two to three times during the summer. It was an opportunity for other churches and parishioners to come together in a convention-type environment. You could see many people within and outside of your congregations. They usually had guest preachers, speakers, and good choirs and singers. There would also be lots of foods from some of the best cooks this side of the Mason-Dixon Line. My brother David and I had no intention of joining the church during this "Revival Week". We went for the entertainment, food, and opportunity to see different folks. My brother and I arrived at church late on the second night of revival week. On this particular evening, we noticed that there were no other seats available but the front row when we entered the sanctuary.

Older parishioners were gracious in encouraging us to take those seats, which we thought had been set-aside for the elderly or the first deacons. They were suspiciously absent this particular night. David initially protested about taking these seats. Later on, we realized that we were sitting on what is commonly referred to as the "mourning bench." These are skillfully planned seats that young people who have not yet joined the church are coerced into sitting on. Skillfully praying church sisters and brothers would be pouring out nonstop prayers and spiritual songs over you. You couldn't help but feel the pressure. Just going up and joining the church would allow you to escape from the heavy hitting praying and singing sisters. You usually just succumbed to the pressure, went up, and made your commitment to Christ, just to get it over with. We both felt that we were pressured into joining. He was fourteen, and I was about twelve. Many church worshippers shared the belief that David was a little overdue and I was right on time.

It was widely understood when you reached your twelfth birthday, you were expected to join the church. After all, everyone knows that this was when Jesus Christ went about His Father's business. David and I were baptized in a tributary of the Mississippi River behind our old church.

As we stood in this big river for baptism dressed in our ceremonial long white robes, I can't say what bothered me more: the dangers that may have been lurking in those deep, dark waters or the mean look on my brother's face. He continued to mutter under his breath: "Why didn't you move like I told you to?" He had such a mean look on his face; I decided to avoid him for several days after our spiritual river renewal.

CHAPTER TWO

Seasoning: Segregation

"You've got to make the Best of a Bad Situation"
(Gladys Knight & the Pips)

Every facet of life in Meridian was segregated or off limits for Negro participation—the neighborhoods, eating establishments, parks, and swimming pools. "White-Only" and "Colored" signs in front of water fountains, bus/ train depot waiting rooms, movie theaters, schools, libraries, golf and tennis courts, and museums surrounded me. There were separate hospital waiting rooms and funeral homes. My mother tried to expose us to as many social/ community opportunities available for blacks as she could for our growth and learning. We had only two television stations, which included PBS on Sunday. We watched and enjoyed classical ballet, and we listen to Italian operas without the understanding of the language. There were few outlets available to us in segregated Meridian, but we were able to combine the beach and family fishing trips a few hours away down on the Gulf Coast. Mother would take us to the zoo in Jackson. She tried to expose us to as many resources available to us in Jim Crow South as she could. My mother also insisted that we participate in 4-H club events and annual state fairs and visit the circus when it came to town. The 4-H club had a heavy emphasis on agriculture and innovative canning. Farming, gardening, and prized cattle and livestock were also valued in my household. At the state fairs, we were able to enjoy our fill of the traditional cotton candy, whirly dip ice cream, corn/chili dogs, and candied apples. The annual circus coming to town exposed us to a world far removed from Mississippi. It provided us an opportunity to be exposed to other people's cultures, customs, foods, and events. My first exposure to listening to European accents was in exchanges between the performers and workers at the state fair/circus. We also tasted many ethnic foods foreign to our taste buds. My mother would often say, "Try it, taste it first, then say that you don't like it. Don't decide without a knowledge base." We saw trampoline and trapeze artists, high-wire cyclists, clowns, and other circus oddities (e.g., bearded ladies; Siamese twins; tall, short, tiny, and fat people). These activities allowed us another eye view to a world beyond the one that we knew in Meridian. We didn't have access to the local community parks, art museums, well-equipped libraries, swimming pools, or restaurants. We didn't have a McDonald's or other fast-food chain that we could access during the sixties in Mississippi. Negroes traveled in their cars and slept in them if they did not have friends or relatives to put them up. The Holiday Inn and other hotels could refuse you lodging, because the 1964 Civil Rights Acts, which provided public accommodation access, had not been passed yet.

Segregation:

One of the tenets of this bill provided equal access to public facilities, which included not being discriminated against for a hotel room. There was no integration of lunch counters, restaurants, et cetera. We could eat in Woolworth at the segregated counter, and we could receive back-door services from a select few little greasy spoons. Colored people chose not to partake because they knew that the food being served to us would be inferior and probably tainted foods.

Train Depot

"People Get Ready, There's a Train A'Comin"
(Curtis Mayfield & The Impressions)

My mother tried to shield us from some of the overt injustices and insults of living in the segregated south.

She would prepare and pack up healthy treats at home before we went on our extended outings in town. She would take us to the train depot's segregated waiting area, and we would take out our little snacks and eat. It was the usual place that we took refuge as we tired from several hours of shopping downtown. After all, who knew that we were not waiting on a distant relative to escort home from the station?

It was comfortable there, and we could daydream and imagine that we were about to embark upon some wonderful train adventure while sitting there. We could watch travelers' come and go, and listen to the loud PA system as departures and destinations were announced. We could watch the passengers and trains leave, taking off to distant places that we could only imagine. We could sit, eat, and revive ourselves without being hassled. Today, I hold a special place in my heart for train travel.

We could attend two of the three movie theaters in our town. The Star Theatre was the only one for Negroes to attend. If we felt courageous enough, we could attend the only integrated theater, the Rhodes (a.k.a. the Rebel). However, very few Negroes attended the Rebel because the seating for the coloreds was relegated to balcony. Most of us could only imagine our fate if a fire broke out. We would be the last to reach the exit. Throughout the city of Meridian, we had to use separate water fountains if we found ourselves thirsty while shopping downtown. The signs were clearly defined. The water fountains for white patrons were clearly labeled White only and for black, Colored Only. The drinking fountains for white were always taller and enclosed within a black-and-silver cooler that made monotonous roaring sounds, and the water flowed as it made a steady returning stream of cool water. I knew that their water was cool because occasionally I would break the rules when I thought that no one was looking.

The colored water fountain was always situated lower. Even as a small child, I recall having to bend down to catch the unsteady stream of usually warm water. It was a single, short often leaky, rusty, and crusty fountain with a small interior bowl and faucet. Just the optics of this mechanism that was designed to provide refreshment and replenishing was an insult to my psychic. It was designed to marginalize and insult, however, I recall feeling more anger about the origin and architect. Why would someone do this to us? I would ask my mother.

There was only one segregated community park that Negroes could attend on the east side of town. Magnolia Park had one swimming pool, a few picnic tables, and a roof-topped canteen with open sides. The colored community would usually bypass two or three well-manicured parks and state-of-the-art swimming pools in order to get to segregated Magnolia Park. I can say the same for the schools in my immediate neighborhood. They were for whites only. I had to walk several blocks away from my home in order to attend one of the centrally located segregated schools for Negroes. As soon as I became old enough to realize the exclusion, it bothered me. I didn't like the feeling of being discriminated against because of my race. I knew that many accepted it and operated in life with this kind of acceptance. However, for me, it felt like an insult to my entire being.

I became more annoyed because I was not able to reconcile racism/segregation with Christianity or religion. My dilemma was: how could God be a liar? I was brought up to believe in God and ascribed to the tenet that He created the world and everything in it. Why would He make one race superior over another? That was not the God that I was taught to serve. The one that said that He created all men in His imagine and all were equal. If the racist whites were right in their feelings of superiority as justification for displacing me, then God was a liar, and I didn't believe God was a liar.

Segregation in Meridian:
I had begun to get angry about the segregated parks, swimming pools, libraries, and museums and especially our assigned black section on the buses/trains, which were divided by the formidable white line. We knew that our section began after the white line on public buses.

White Woman's Kitchen

"What's Gonna On?" (Marvin Gaye)

When I reached the age of fourteen, I took a Saturday job with a white woman who appeared rather guilt-stricken. She hired me to do ironing and light cleaning for her on Saturday. She was employed in a large shirt factory where shirts were manufactured, and she ironed for a living. I have to admit, I was never really good at ironing, and I'm sure that she recognized that fact. I would engage in other kitchen duties: arranging the chairs, setting the table, and pouring the sweet tea or lemonade. Chores included supervising the food that she prepared, light cleaning like dusting, stirring a pot or two, but she never really required me to cook, just check on things on the stove. It was a pleasant arrangement, and I was paid a dollar an hour, which was considered adult wages in those days. I noticed that she seemed to enjoy my company. I sometimes wondered why she paid me to do work. It appeared that I had another inferred job as her manicurist and a lunch date, provided she had no white company. She would often share a meal and conversation with me at her table. She would talk a lot, and I would usually just listen. I remember her polishing my fingernails and her teaching me to polish her nails. As a matter of fact, she was the first person to polish my nails. She had no children, and I noticed that her husband was rarely home, even though this was the weekend. Sometimes, she would have friends stop by, and I knew my place when they came over. I had to leave the kitchen table and go toward the back of the kitchen, where there was a separate little wooden table for me to sit and finish my meal. I finished the cleaning in a timely fashion; however, my ironing skills were lacking. It appeared that I wasn't fast enough for her. Since she worked in a shirt factory, and she was really fast with ironing. Most days, she'd end up helping me with my assigned ironing task. She seemed most interested in me finishing fast so she could have me sit with her and do nails. When her friends would drop by unexpectedly, I'd have to get up and pretend that I was doing chores that were already completed. Years later, I discovered the source of her apparent guilt. Her husband came home early one day and caught her with her black lover. The two had been carrying on the affair for years before being caught. Her black lover was sentenced to prison for this alleged rape. Her lover lived in the same neighborhood on a street that paralleled my employer's. Her home bordered the colored section of town called the East End. It was not unusual in the South to have whites and blacks living in what appeared to be the same neighborhood. Streets or blocks could separate blacks and whites. Negroes and whites in Meridian could live in the same neighborhood but not on the same street. My employer's black lover could reach her home often by just walking through his backyard into her back door, and they carried on their illicit arrangement for years until they were caught. When her husband caught them, she cried rape. I later discovered that the black community had been aware of their clandestine romance for years and remained silent. I also discovered that she was unable to get any black help in the surrounding area. They refused to work for this white woman who had caused this black man's false imprisonment. I understand that her spouse never really bought the "rape story." He only went along in order to protect her honor. This probably accounted for his frequent absence or marginal interaction with my employer within the home. I could not help notice that his interactions with her were rare and often appeared hostile.

Striking Out on My Own

"We shall not be moved"

My desire to change things grew out of my dissatisfaction with segregated life in Mississippi and my own feelings that there was inherently something wrong with one group of people (God's people) being privileged over the other. A strong sense of fairness seemed to be just a part of my DNA.

Fighting injustice just seemed so natural to me. When things just didn't seem right, I courageously took chances, sometimes without thinking of the consequences. I was keenly aware that every facet of life in Mississippi was segregated or off limits for black participation. I am sure Rosa Parks, the Birmingham bus boycott, and the Greensboro students influenced me, as did reading Ebony and Jet magazines about the stands students were taking all over the South. I decided one day to take it upon myself to singlehandedly test the climate of Meridian's segregated bus system. On this particular Saturday afternoon, I had just completed my maid services for my "nice white lady" who lived on the wrong side of town. I went out to my bus stop to wait for the bus that would take me home. My ride would take would take approximately forty-five minutes. When the bus arrived at my stop, I got on the bus as usual.

But I just decided not to sit in the assigned colored section. I couldn't get over feeling demeaned, marginalized, and less than a human being. I paid like everyone else, and I should be able to sit wherever I pleased.

The section was clearly defined by that god-awful white line. Oh god, how I hated that line of delineation! I got onto the bus and sat in the front section that was set aside for whites only. I took this forbidden seat filled with all the panic and fear that a teenage body could endure but sat there anyway. After a while, I felt transfixed and frozen. I don't believe that I could have moved if I wanted to. I sat there strained, sweaty, and overcome with panic and fear concerning my fate, just waiting for what was to come next. Then I heard the voice of the white bus driver, which sounded like thunder cutting through a storm. It broke the raging silence: "Gal, what do you think that you are doing?" He spoke twice, and I ignored him. "Gal?" Still no response. Then I heard another familiar voice coming from the back of the bus.

It was the familiar voice of my sharp-tongued aunt Essie, who was riding on the same bus. I'd recognize that hoarse and raspy voice of hers anywhere. She had taken the same bus as she was headed home from her Saturday employer. She began to caution me to move to the back to my place in the designated black section. I didn't turn around to look at her, and kept my face and body facing forward. She began encouraging me to come to the back along with several other colored patrons, who were apparently getting upset. They all began to complain, yell, and cajole me. They told me to get up and move to my place in the back of the bus. Perhaps, the bus driver was trying to give my black people the opportunity to get me to cooperate. He stopped making his demands in deference to them getting me to cooperate. I noticed that after they began to come on so hot and heavy, he ceased with his warning toward me. I can't tell you what was operating that caused me to take such a courageous action on my own that day. I wouldn't be able to explain it today. All I know is that I had to take that spontaneous risk. I continued to remain in my seat sweating and petrified with fear. My aunt and other blacks began to apply more verbal pressure. I later realized what I initially considered as anger was fear. They were frightened, not only for me, but also for themselves. I began to feel more frightened for them and the repercussions from my aunt than that of the driver and other white patrons, who seemed to have frozen in angry silence.

I finally acquiesced by just moving one row back, which placed me on the border of the black-and-white delineation line. My stop was approaching, and I gladly got off, avoiding the anticipated wrath from both blacks and whites. Aunt Essie made a special visit to my home to tell my father, "That girl is going to get us all killed. You'd better watch her."

School/Religion:

I was lucky during part of my fifth and sixth grade years to live near Wechsler Elementary, which was only a few blocks from my home. Upon entering junior high, I had to walk several miles to attend an all-black school. I passed several neighborhood schools for white students en route to the all-black school. As soon as I became old enough to realize the exclusion, it bothered me. I didn't like the feeling of being discriminated against or inconvenienced just against because of my race. I knew that many accepted it and operated in life with this kind of acceptance. However, for me, it always felt like a nagging insult that permeated my entire being. It was a feeling that I found hard to shake. I had many discussions with my mother. She listened and identified with the pain that I felt. She always cautioned us not to hate and to restrain from judging all whites the same way. She used to say by doing that, you are cooperating with the enemy, and you end up no different than your oppressor. She tried to humor me with stories about Christ and the dangers of becoming like your oppressors. I wondered about the song that I was taught in Sunday school, was that a lie too? "Jesus loves the little children, all the children of the world. Red and yellow, black and white, they are precious in His sight. Jesus loves the little children of the world." I thought that all children were taught this song at a young age. I felt that anyone who would go through such means to prevent someone from having freedoms that should have been their natural birthright granted by God had a mental illness. I was not able to reconcile racism and discrimination with my Christians beliefs.

School Life

Each year in Meridian, the best student artists were selected from the Negro high schools, and given the opportunity to paint Halloween scenes on the windows of the better department stores. Many students competed and their art was judged and prized annually. My brothers, David and Marshall, always took away the first and second prizes respectively. It was commonly understood that one of the Sims's brothers would take away the coveted prize. Since the better stores wanted the best artwork displayed on their windows, my brother's participation in subsequent years were just requested for this annual event. It became apparent to me that the only time that whites in Mississippi demonstrated any appreciation for *colored* could be observed in sports or the arts. They could easily demonstrate pride in the fact that *International Opera great*, Leontyne Price, hails from Laurel, Mississippi.

At an early age, I resigned myself for years to think that artistic skills were a male trait in my family. At the same time, we knew that the talent came from my mother's lineage. She won many trophies and awards for floral arrangements, artwork, fashion designs, food preparation, and raising superior livestock.

My early civics classes set the tone and created my love for history, government, and patriotism for my county. Each morning, my classmates and I recited the pledge of allegiance to the flag of the United States of America. We proudly stood in our classroom with one hand placed across our hearts, saying with much conviction: "I pledge allegiance to the flag of the United States of America and to the republic for which it stands, one nation, under God, indivisible, with liberty and justice for all." I developed a love for government in my social studies and civics classes in junior high school. I do believe that this love of those subjects laid an additional foundation for more seeds of unrest and pride to sprout. In these history classes, I learned about the three branches of government and how they interacted with each other in order to form a more perfect union—a system of government providing checks and balances to make a fair and equitable government for its entire people. In a democratic society, I learned that we all could enjoy life, liberty, and the pursuit of happiness. I believed that our government was a government of the people, for the people, and by the people. I remember being fueled by memorization of the Declaration of Independence and the Gettysburg Address. We also learned the importance of the Bill of Rights of the Constitution of the United States and all those beautiful lyrics of "The Star-Spangled Banner" and "America the Beautiful" and my favorite poem: "America for Me" by Henry Van Dyke.

'Tis fine to see the Old World, and travel up and down among the famous palaces and cities of renown, to admire the crumbly castles and the statues of the kings—But now I think I've had enough of antiquated things. So it's home again, and home again, America for me! My heart is turning home again, and there I long to be, In the land of youth and freedom beyond the ocean bars—Where the air is full of sunlight and the flag is full of stars! America for me!

I recall during an election period, our entire school became involved in the election process. Classrooms were set up to represent each state and its electoral vote. This was done in order to reinforce the Electoral College system and how we elected our president. Each classroom represented a state in the union. We ran races to include the primaries, state, and national election offices. The entire student body became involved in electing the candidates to run for all offices, including the presidential race. We made speeches based upon our platform, and the student body voted. Ultimately, we elected our president and vice president, senators, congressmen, et cetera. I recall that the candidates who won the largest amount of votes based upon the Electoral College system became the president of our student body. We learned and were challenged by our ability to memorize and recite excerpts from the Gettysburg Address: "Four scores and seven years ago, our forefathers brought forth on this continent a new nation conceived in liberty and dedicated to the proposition that all men are created equal. Now we are engaged in a great civil war, testing whether that nation, or any nation, so conceived and so dedicated, can long endure. We are met on a great battlefield of that war. We have come to dedicate a portion of that field, as a final resting place for those who here gave their lives that that nation might live. It is altogether fitting and proper that we should do this." Our Declaration of Independence, which says that: "We holds these truths to be self-evident that all men are created equal." We learned about the Constitution of the United States of America. We learned about the Thirteenth, Fourteenth, Eighteenth, and Nineteenth Amendments (the abolishment of slavery, the right to vote, and women's suffrage). These amendments as I understood them were put in place to correct the wrongs and consider the forgotten/overlooked. I loved learning about the different political parties and studying the various forms of government. I thrived on the separation of power and learning about the justice system. I did not believe that we could have had a more perfect union. One of my favorite songs was "The Star-Spangled Banner" by Francis Scott Key. All the words took on a special meaning when I learned how and when he wrote it, not knowing whether he would even see the sunlight again. He wrote it in the middle of the War of 1812 while watching his surroundings being destroyed by bombs bursting in air. Singing "my country 'tis of thee, sweet land of liberty" could bring tears to my eyes. I loved and absorbed civics, history, and government. I learned in my history classes about the grandfather clause, unfair poll taxes, Northern and Southern racism, and segregation and oppression in other countries. I was encouraged upon learning about the large numbers of legislative seats won by blacks in Mississippi after the Reconstruction period. Mississippi had the largest number of blacks elected to state legislatures and as representatives of any state years after that period. I was especially disturbed about the various methods of intimidation, including Northern and Southern lynching's to discourage blacks when they had acquired some gains after the Reconstruction period. I grew even angrier over the tactics to intimate and deny blacks a voice in their freedoms. My mother agreed that segregation and discrimination were wrong and didn't coincide with Christianity. I had many talks with my maternal grandfather, who seemed to agree that segregation and white superiority was evil, mean-spirited, and self-centered, based upon power and greed. My mother's focus was on ignorance, love, and forgiveness. She always encouraged us to surrender all problems to God and let Him be the judge. My maternal grandfather, Dennis held different views. He felt that southern whites feared losing their place in society. He said that if Negroes were given the same education, rights, and privileges that were allotted to whites simply by their birthright, subsequently, blacks could excel and compete with whites on a level playing field.

Granddaddy:
We were led to believe that his real father probably abandoned my granddaddy. A white family raised him along with two siblings who were allegedly related to him. Granddaddy's appearance was ethnically ambiguous, and much

23

of his origin remains a mystery. He ran the *family store* while my mother was a toddler. I recalled that he continued to run this sundry store when I begin my first grade of school in Meridian. After we moved, we would always return for country visits to *granddaddy's store*. My sibs and I could always depend upon my Grandfather Dennis's generosity on certain days of the week. We knew that we could count on getting extra popsicles, ice cream bars, root beer, peach; strawberry sodas, and endless supplies of root beer and assorted flavored candy canes. The move to Meridian when I reached about 5 meant that I would be attending the city school for the first grade. I never thought of him as looking white until many years later, when a young classmate expressed confusion about his ethnic identity. My friend Ethel came by for an after school visit to teach me how to tell time. Ethel came by my home with a big clock with moveable hands to assist me in my learning. Earlier at school, we both discovered that I could not tell time. She was busily teaching me about the clock and reinforcing a math lesson. She and I were sitting on the porch at our new home when Granddaddy Dennis made one of his weekly visits. When Ethel saw my granddaddy emerged from the front door, my tutoring friend stopped cold, bringing my lesson to a halt. I begin to cajole her to finish what she had started in my playful seven-year-old demeanor. She just seemed transfixed by my grandfather. I continued to play at learning the clock and did my usual interaction with my grandfather. It was only after he had completed his weekly visit and walked away from our home when Ethel regained her focus. She quickly turned to me and asked me a question that I have pondered for years. She asked: "Why do ya'll have that white man visiting your house?" I thought that her comment was incredulous and her observation was ridiculous, and I laughed as I said, "Are you crazy? That's no white man, that's my granddaddy!" It took me years to comprehend her confusion.

I know that my granddaddy considered himself an expert on the southern white man's behavior. I just knew that he was an authority because he would usual start his conversation about them with: "Now let me tell you about the southern white man". It appeared that his education was reinforced by listening to their late-night conversations through cracks in his bedroom walls. He heard many conversations where whites plotted and devised ways to suppress black progress with unfair shareholding tactics, especially those who demonstrated some independence and freedom from the constraints of Jim Crow and tenant farming. "They thought that I was asleep, he said". I could hear them talking through the walls about ways to take back their land. They would discuss overcharging them, and other abusive tactics. Sharecropping was very common in the south. Negro family living on the white landowners' property would be charged rent; the family farmed and worked his land that accumulated crop value. The Negro family was given a small portion of the crops for personal use. They were never paid for their work. They stayed in a perpetual state of being always in debt with the landholder. By the time the landowners deducted rent for lodging, water, oil, fertilizer, seeds for planting, cotton expenses, etc. The sharecropper could never be released from his debt to the landholder. The sharecropper debt was never paid, and he remained disenfranchised forever. They had no real freedoms. If they attempted to exercise any freedoms of independence in property ownership, co-op farming or work coordination with other sharecroppers, they would be discouraged with threats of violence or lynching. He knew that they would do whatever necessary to keep the negroes/niggahs) in line. "Getting out of line" could be interpreted as any act where the Negro made any attempt to advance themselves: Register to vote or hold onto their inherited property. Granddaddy grew up with them, but developed a deep-seated distrust for their unscrupulous business practices and maltreatment of Negroes. I just knew that he was an authority on "all these southern white bastards". He'd often say, they'll cut off their nose to spite their own face." "He will stomp on his own mother to keep a niggahs from getting ahead." I somehow trusted his wisdom. After all, he'd tell me, "why I have lived and "worked around 'em for most of his life". I also discovered my grandfather held a special resentment for the so-call "G-men". He seemed to associate most of his business failures directly on the lap of these mysterious G-men. I later discovered that the G- stood for government workers during prohibition. These G-Men work assignment involved eradicating the stills, sale, and use of illegal whisky. During the prohibition period, they would go into rural and small town's countryside seeking out and destroying illegal whisky plants (still mills). It appeared that my granddaddy had encountered them in the south while they were on their job. My grandfather had a thriving side business selling cars and moonshine Whisky.

The manufacturing of moonshine whisky in secluded places had long been a profitable sideline for local farmers in Legally "dry" Mississippi.' Some of these G-men located and destroyed several of granddaddy's still mills located throughout rural Meridian and Lauderdale County. One could always engage Granddaddy Dennis into negative conversations about these greedy G-men. It seemed that the thought of them could turn his stomach *raw* with their pervasive, intrusive behavior. The local police had a "don't ask, look for, and don't tell policy about whisky stills. Granddaddy was said to be related to most of them, so he wasn't too concerned about interference from the locals, the G-men, however, was another story.

He often said that whites' fears were based upon a need to feel superior and have someone to look down on—especially the uneducated ones. Southern whites have been known to use the Bible to justify abuse of blacks because we are said to be the descendants of Ham. The Bible speaks of Ham's descendants in the Old Testament. During one of Noah's off times, he got drunk and exposed his nakedness as he lay among his vineyard. One son discovered this sight, told his brother, and made fun of his father. The other brother went out and covered his father nakedness with a blanket. He walked away from his father walking backward with his eyes closed as he covered his father. When Noah awoke from his wine stupor, and found out what his youngest son had done to him, he said, "Cursed be Canaan! The lowest of slaves will he be to his brothers" (Genesis 9:25).

My experience with whites in the South was limited. In the relationships between blacks and whites in the South, it always appeared that blacks had to be subservient to whites. After all, Southern whites spent most of their time making sure black people were suppressed in every way: economically, socially, educationally, etc.

When the movement came to my home in Meridian, Mississippi, I was attracted to it like a bee to honey and like a moth to a flame, but I really didn't know if the Mississippi movement came to me or if it had ignited something already in me.

My mother agreed that Jim Crow didn't coincide with true Christian principles. She agreed that there were many contradictions and hypocrisies based in ignorance, fear, and insecurity. My grandfather labeled it as evil, mean-spirited, and self-centered, based on upon power and greed. We had many conversations about my discontent over racism and segregation in the south. If one is privileged, then you develop a sense of entitlement. They expected it because they had always been the beneficiaries of the freedoms that others have had to struggle or fight for. I remember a scene that was deeply etched in my mind while watching the Television news about the desegregation of the Little Rock Schools. I watched as the US Marshalls were escorting nine children to school. I saw angry mobs of students and adults holding racist signs, throwing bottles and cans, and hurtling insults toward these students. A TV reporter interviewed an angry white woman as she explained on camera her reasons she didn't want blacks to get an equal access to education. She looked into the camera and said, "If they get the same education as whites, then who will we have to look down on?"

Growing up, my mother would always inject a broader point of view that was more balanced. She would never allow us to say all white people were evil. Her corrections would be, say some, not all. She would often give examples of how the opposite was true. Never think that all black people are your friend either, you must learn to accept people as people, and let their actions be your judge. At times, I could not hold onto her objective way of seeing things when she provided examples of goodness from southern white people. She was motivated by love, I thought to a fault at times. She cautioned us not to hate when we talked about how evil the southern white man was. My mother also reminded us that when she was only two and my aunt was a baby that they were taken care of by a white family. Her mother died in childbirth, and they needed care while my granddaddy worked in a "family" store until he remarried. So my mother cautioned us not to put all whites in the same category. She always cautioned against our hating all white people. This was a tough pill to swallow in the Jim Crow Mississippi growing up in the 1950 and 60's. They seemed to be our enemies on every turn.

My mother warned us against joining the "enemy." She expounded on the virtues of Christianity and warned how hate could only destroy the person who holds onto it. She also found many ways to illustrate an idea. Whenever my younger sibling and I would get into fights as children, she was bothered by the anger that we held for each other after the fight and our whippings.

She came to me one day, gave me a nickel, and told me to hold it as tight as I could between two fingers (my thumb and third finger). She stood nearby, instructing me to hold onto the nickel harder and harder. She kept insisting that I try to hold even harder, but after a while, I had to drop the nickel because it became too painful between my two red, raw fingers. It was such a relief just to let it go, because holding it longer and harder only hurt me, not the nickel. I guess I got her point. I still felt instinctively that something was very wrong with one set of human beings standing in the way of another and preventing them from obtaining what was rightfully theirs in the first place. I thought that only God, the Declaration of Independence, and the Constitution could grant these rights.

CHAPTER THREE

Pre-Freedom Summer

"I heard it Through the Grapevine" (Gladys Knight & the Pips)

During the summer of 1963, our NAACP youth group had visited Medgar Evers's church for a rally. We heard a dynamic speaker from Maryland who was then National Director Mitchell of the NAACP. He talked about the impending Freedom Summer and the initiative that was on its way. We were so excited and fired up for what was to come and wanted to be a part of this effort to help get our civil rights and freedoms. A group of about eight of us left Medgar Evers's church to have lunch at his home. His wife, Myrlie, had prepared fried chicken, peas, carrots, mashed potatoes, and Jell-O for dessert. I didn't know it at the time that I was seated at the same table where Medgar had renegotiated his civil rights plans for continued fearless involvement in a movement that was threatening his life. I was seated at the table where he cautioned his wife and elicited her full commitment. I sat in the same home where he had introduced parlor games to his children that reinforced safety procedures in the event they were threatened with violence in their home. I used their bathroom, which his family had collectively decided would provide a safety zone. I understood that Mr. Evers devised emergency and safety plans to protect his family through those parlor games he played with his children.

Mr. Evers was aware at that time that there had been threats against his life. He was attempting to prepare and protect his children with game scenarios about the safest place in the house to go if something happened. I didn't know it at the time that I was sitting within arm range of their home safety zone. I was in his home on a Sunday afternoon in the spring of 1963 having lunch. He would be gunned down a few feet from where I sat in his living room just weeks later. He was assassinated in front of his garage on June 12, 1963. The Evers home and neighborhood is now a civil rights memorial site in Jackson, Mississippi.

Fall 1963, JFK

"Come See About Me" (The Supremes)

Five months later, on November 22, 1963, around my lunchtime, members of our youth group were quietly summoned to the high school principal's office. We were also under the impression that our activism had been kept quiet because we never spoke about it outside of our group. When some of our classmates became aware of our nonviolent activities, we were often teased about our commitment to the teachings of Gandhi and Martin Luther King Jr. I recognized that everyone being called in was a member of our NAACP youth group. We were taken to a large conference room that I never knew existed. I became concerned about possibly being expelled. The previous principal had expelled James Chaney for wearing an NAACP paper button on her shirt. During the course of this sequester, we learned that President John F. Kennedy had been assassinated in Dallas, Texas, while riding in a convertible with his wife Jacqueline Beauvoir Kennedy and the governor of Texas and his wife. We heard that Governor Conyers had also been wounded. When we reached home that evening, we watched the national news and heard more details. We watched the usually stoic newsman Walter Cronkite fight back tears as he reported the news. It was as if the lifeblood had been drained from the world. We subsequently heard that Conyers's wife asked, "Are they going to kill us all?" Because she heard more than one shot fired. We learned on that day that our principal wasn't as cool, aloof, and unfeeling as he had led us to believe. He wanted to give us an opportunity to express our feelings about the news of the president's death. He allowed us to ventilate our feelings about his death and assess our safety fears. I recalled that there was no rush to have us return to class and we remained sequestered in this room for most of the day. We were not permitted to go home until family members could be contacted to escort us, and if no one was home, a school assistant took us home. Many of us in those days did not have a telephone in the home. If parents could not be located, the principal provided us with escorts to get us home for the day. He was more aware of our activities than we had thought. We remained secretive about our extracurricular activities and usually only talked within our group. He had heard about some of us being under attack by white thugs who threw rocks and tomatoes at us while we protested in our efforts to integrate some downtown stores. I was hit on my arm by a large rock as I ducked, using my arm to protect my face. I remember going to the police to report the incident, which involved five white teenage boys whom I could identify. The policeman on duty simply looked at me with a cold response and broke out in laughter when we left.

I felt stunned and shocked with a pervading feeling of disappointment over the loss of our "liberal" president. We wondered what this meant to the movement with the loss of our biggest supporter and what would happen to us as a people. As some of us were leaving the school, other students stared at us, some making various comments: "That's those civil rights fighters; they must be in trouble." We were moved by the reaction of our principal, whom we had once thought of as coldhearted, tough, and unfeeling. The local white town people in Meridian took this opportunity to throw a parade complete with rebel flags, ugly signs of hatred, as they used whistles, car horns, and noise-makers in celebrations upon the death of our beloved President. They flooded the streets with loud cars in gaiety, speeches and song. I was overcome with confused grief as I remembered a lot about slain leader Medgar Evers this sad day. My family and I were devastated that there was so much hate for the leader of our world. I wondered how we must be viewed internationally. I made an association between the assassination of Lincoln and President Kennedy. Both appeared to be acts of violence against leaders whose motivation were toward equal rights for black people. The Emancipation Proclamation that would end slavery and The Civil Rights Bill ending segregation and providing free assets for blacks. Removing obstacles to their being able to walk free in this world. I wondered a lot about the relationship between violence and black people's freedoms and civil rights.

Our NAACP Surrogates: Albert Jones, Charles Young, and Charles Darden introduced us to Matt Suarez (Flukie). Matt was an experienced field worker who had been active in Canton, Ms. He was handsome with caramel colored skin and most of the girls developed a crush on him. He had a devil make care laugh, and appeared very confident which rubbed off on us. By the time I was sixteen, my brothers and I were active in the youth branch of the NAACP under the leadership of Charles Darden who was Medgar Evers's Co–Field Secretary for the state of Mississippi. We were a tightly knit group that held monthly meetings to discuss strategies for desegregation, voter registration, and racial equality. Charles Darden put our youth group up to canvassing door-to-door, urging black adults to register to vote. We knocked on doors, but most people would shut the door in our faces. "I am not interested in that kind of junk," echoed among the black citizens that we did contact. We were relentless and continued to push because we thought that we were fighting for our very own lives. The idea of exclusion became more and more unpalatable. We knew what it was like to get doors slammed in our faces by blacks in our own community. We knew we had to start with them, get them on board, and help them to appreciate a life without segregation and discrimination. Their resistance did not deter us; it became a challenge to us to try to win over a few converts.

The surrogates had decided that the safest way to test the early waters of desegregation and civil rights would be to use the already seasoned youth in Meridian. After all, we had already been out there in the struggle for equality.

We knew what it was like to get doors slammed in our faces. Many times, after leaving church services, we would engage in protest marches, which took the format of silent marches with protest signs or singing songs of protest.

We went to small businesses that were frequented by Negroes but had no Negro employees. We would carry handmade protest signs as we often marched in silence, and other times singing freedom songs:

"Ain't Gonna Let No Body Turn Me Round, Turn Me Round, Turn me round, Ain't Gonna Let Bull Conner Turn me Round, Turn me Round, Turn me Round, Gonna Keep on a marchin, Keep on Aprayin, Marching up Freedom's Way.".

"We shall not, we shall not be moved, just like a tree that's planted by the water, We shall not be moved."

"Oh Freedom, Oh Freedom, Oh Freedom Over me, Over me, and before I'll be a slave, I'll be buried in my grave, and go home to my Lord and be free." No more suffering, No more dying, over me, over me, and before I'll be a slave, I'll be buried in my grave, and go home to my Lord and be Free.

"Blowing in the Wind"- How many roads must a man walk down before he is called a man. The answer my friend is blowing in the wind, the answer is blowing in the wind."

"This Little Light of Mine": I'm gonna let it shine, This little light of mine, I'm gonna let it shine, Let it shine, shine, shine, let it shine."

We would always join hands crossed in front and usually ended with our standard:

"We Shall Overcome, We Shall Overcome, We Shall Overcome someday A A A A, OH OH Deep In My Heart, I Do Believe, We Shall Overcome Some day. God is on our Sides; God is on our side today AAAAAAAAh. Ooooh Deep in My Heart, I Do Believe, We Shall Overcome Some Day."

We often started and ended our meetings singing Freedom Songs that provided us with inspiration and motivation. We saw our involvement as another way that we could express ourselves. We lived in a community that offered few if any organized activities for black youth.

It was during our NAACP youth group meeting that we heard about the plans for the upcoming Mississippi Summer Project. We later learned that the city's black clergy had called a meeting to discuss how they could support COFO. It was via our NAACP youth involvement that we first heard about the "Calvary" (freedom workers) coming to help us in the summer of 1964. I like, most of the black youth who filled the movement's ranks, was less timid. We saw our involvement in the civil rights movement as a means of tackling head-on the social conditions that had made life difficult for us in the South. We were introduced to another surrogate, Reverend Charles Johnson who started his church in our neighborhood. We were encouraged to visit his church by our established surrogates: the photographer Charles Darden. We found that Reverend Johnson offered an alternative to the hellfire-and-brimstone sermons that we had grown accustomed to. He came from out of state and did not seem to resign himself to it the way other blacks in the state did. He appeared to be more of a maverick and in touch with the progressive nature of teens. We didn't know it at the time, but he was to play an instrumental role in the early stages of the civil rights movement in Meridian. We didn't discover until years later that he had a run-in with Klan members upon his arrival in Meridian. Some of the same Klan members later took part in the murder of Chaney, Goodman, and Schwerner.

"How many road must a man walk down before you call him a man, the answer my friend is Blowing in the wind" (Bob Dylan)

"Reverend Charles Johnson and his family came to Meridian in 1963. The morning of their arrival, Johnson and his wife toured the city by car and were depressed by their first glimpse of the black precincts west of town and by the rigid Jim Crow segregation they observed along the city's main shopping streets. That afternoon, Reverend Johnson returned downtown alone to mail a letter to his supervisor reporting his safe arrival. Heading east on Eighth Street, he saw an angled parking place in front of the post office and, making a wide turn, swung his car around into it. As he stepped out of the car, a policeman came running out of the barbershop across the street. The officer, cursing, leveled a massive revolver at Johnson's temple. "You don't do that here, nigger," the officer told him, "or I'll blow your brains out." Johnson was given to understand he had committed a traffic violation. The young minister stood with his hands against the car and the cop's gun at his head. Across the street, a group of white men were standing in the barbershop doorway, shouting, "Kill him, Lee! Kill him!"

"He could squeeze the trigger," Johnson later recalled thinking, "and my obituary would read, 'Shot while resisting arrest.'" It had happened like that to countless other blacks. Thankfully, the officer seemed to be feeling merciful that day and let Johnson off with a warning. The young minister quickly learned his way around town. That particular barbershop, Bill Gordon's, he was told, was a popular redneck handout. A black man passed by there only if he had to and then with extreme caution. As for the cop who had held the gun to his head, he was named Lee Roberts, and he too was to be avoided. Roberts and a brother named Wayne were "mean as yard dogs," prime Ku Klux Klan material. Wayne Roberts (a Klan member involved in the murders of Chaney, Goodman, and Schwerner) would later become one of Sam Bower's most eager recruits. ("We Are Not Afraid by Seth Cagin & Phillip Dray),"

CHAPTER FOUR

The Movement Comes Home

Charles R. Darden, our NAACP leader put our youth group up to canvassing door-to-door, urging black adults to register to vote. We received much resistance, however, it didn't curtail our efforts. Their resistance did not deter us; it became a challenge to us to try to win over a few converts. We discovered that Rev Johnson was also was more socially active as he begun to recognize and expose cases of spousal and child abuse, which was a taboo subject during these times. He dared to bring local media attention in efforts to protect abused victims and innocent children. It was only then that my mother forgave me for dissing my prior church when she recognized the good that he was providing for the community. She also realized my affection for this church was not a personal attack upon her rearing or an affront to her religious directions. Initially, I got into trouble with my mother who thought that I was neglecting my former church. I tried to explain to my mother why I liked Rev Johnson's church. He was different, he actually taught the bible in a way that I understood. She reluctantly approved of my giving up my Baptist church, but not without a battle. She eventually resigned herself the fact that in my family history, there were Methodists; I told her that the church of the Nazarene was a form of Methodist. She remembered that her grandmother was a Methodist, so this eased the temperature in my home. She also noticed that my group and I were committed, and we attended on a regular bases. Our Surrogates: Darden, Jones, and Johnson had decided that the safest way to test the early desegregation waters and civil rights would be done by the already seasoned youth of Meridian. After all, we had already been out there in the struggle for equality. Matt Suarez, the seasoned Field Worker from Canton, Ms. educated us with an overview of Freedom Summer and we understood the desegregation and voter's registration component.

We learned that other Freedom workers would be coming to Meridian to provide addition services to our cause by setting up a community center, Freedom School, and CORE Office. We subsequently learned that CORE workers Michael and Rita Schwerner would be spearheading these efforts. Our Surrogates explained to us the goals of Freedom Summer and expressed a need for our help. We had gone to homes throughout many rural communities and collected paper ballots with our Surrogate, Flukie. Some of these ballots were signed by the letter X, from those citizens who were illiterate, and would later participate in literacy programs at the community centers.

These marked ballots that we collected represented a significant voice, as we understood it. These ballots would represent black people whose voice has been silenced for a long time. These protest votes would be saying in effect: "I am entitled to vote as citizen of the U.S. and you have unfair Jim Crows laws serving as Barriers. These barriers are standing in the way of my rights as a human being and citizen of the US. I would be voting if not for the obstacles that you as a state have placed upon me. "Here is my voice anyway, I am silent no more". These ballots were designed to play a larger role to oppose and unseat the regular Mississippi Delegates from the state. They were put into place to give our plight a voice so that the nation could hear during the 1964 Democratic Convention to be held in August 1964. We believed in what we were doing, and I know that we were oblivious to the danger of being caught and lynched. We had no fear, there seemed to be raw courage and power in unity. Some of the roads that we took were dangerous after dark, but it was the only time people would talk. My brother, Marshall was trained as field representative for COFO initiatively before J.E received the assignment. He and David used to drive the notorious civil right station wagon. Marshall left for NY after high school under the duress of constant harassment by the police. My parent had to bail them out of jail on several occasions. The police, however, was unable to distinguish my brothers apart, so when arrested, the officer would ask them: "Who do I have this time, David or is this Marshall? One evening as Marshall was stopped at a red light while unwrapping a piece of candy, he got arrested. He asked the officer what were the charges, and the respond was: "vagrancy". Vagrancy was a catchall charge for many arrests of civil rights workers.

During the fall of 1963, we would accompany Flukie on some of these "missions". We understood that the goal was to collect votes from registered and unregistered black voters. Our efforts were called direct canvassing which took place "in the field" (away from home), at churches, community centers, cafe', wherever we could solicit cooperation. Our early involvement with the NAACP had already earned our group a repetition within the community. We were unaware that we would be the sacrificial lambs to test the early waters of Civil Rights Movement in Meridian. We agreed to things that we had not fully understood. We had already participated in several protest marches for equal employment at restaurants, Department stores, and utility plants. Our involvements consisted of sit-ins, sing-ins, and several silent protest marches where carried signs of protest against segregated establishments. After the Freedom schools/community centers established, the work would continue there. As part of our outreach, we canvassed in rural areas where there was usually no electricity. We tried to complete our "field" or mission activities before dark. If we found ourselves out after sundown in some rural poorly lit countryside, our fearless leader, Flukie would drive fast and reckless in direction of home.

Michael and Rita Schwerner were among the first Freedom Summer recruits to arrive in Meridian in their little Volkswagen Beetle in January 1964. They were with CORE initially. Later on, civil rights organizations combined to what we came to know as COFO (Congress of Federated Organizations) to include CORE, SNCC, SCLC, and NAACP.

Although, we were not age appropriate yet, we gained honorary membership in COFO because we were members of the youth branch of the NAACP.

Mickey and Rita spent a lot of time at our home. My mother and Mickey hit it off right away. Mother like the idea that he was a little chubby in the middle. She called him healthy and he loved her cooking. Our house became known as one of the host homes for newly arriving freedom fighters coming to Meridian. My father had a union job, so he was not subjected to a lot of the harassment or job threats that many in our town encountered. Many of the new recruits who arrived in Meridian were welcomed into our home. My mother applauded the movement and the role that they would be playing in voter registration and desegregation. She was aware of the negative press that they were receiving in the local media and some governmental officials. Freedom workers were being criticized for their uniform and dress code. The freedom workers wore denim naturally for its durability. They were accused of being dirty because many looked the same in this chosen denim uniform. My mother was always concerned about the overall image and personal hygiene of the fighters. The number of racist, insulting remarks made by the press and our then governors of Mississippi and Alabama fueled her concern. My mother always allowed any of the volunteers to use our washer to launder their clothing anytime that they came by. The freedom workers well-established denim uniform, which provided comfort and durability for fieldwork. It consisted of T-shirts and blue jean tops and bottoms. Both governors and other racists in power accused the freedom fighters of being smelly and dirty. They were called dirty, agitators, whoremongers, infidels, etc. My mother didn't want "bad things" being said about these wonderful young people. These brave people were making such wonderful sacrifices for a *"good cause."* She devised a plan to get them to take a bath without making them feel bad or insulted. She would tell them, "Now, while I am warming up your food or preparing your dinner, you will have time to go in and relax in a hot tub of water in the bathroom that I have drawn up for you. By the time that you get finished, your supper will be ready."

At our house, the new recruits could find short-term lodging and get their haircut, a warm meal, and a hot bath a la Mommy Sims. Word got around quickly that my brothers were good at cutting all hair types. The white recruits could not go to the white barbershops downtown. If they attempted to, they would immediately be rejected and harassed as soon as they opened their mouths. Their accents would be a dead giveaway, and they would be subjected to rejection and humiliation. They were called Northern agitators.

"Are you one of those agitators coming down here to disrupt our way of life and getting the niggahs stirred up? You ole Jew bastards better get the hell outta here iff'an you knows what good for you!" was the response, along with other obscenities and directions.

D-Day

In Meridian, we had several five- and ten-cent stores that blacks frequented often. Kress, Woolworth's, and Newberry's stores sold heavily to blacks but refused to hire black salesclerks. Under the leadership of Mickey, we decided upon a boycott with two primary demands: that they hire blacks as clerks and desegregate lunch counters. We selected a day that we referred to as D-Day, being the target date for the boycott. We had actively passed out flyers in the black community informing them of the planned boycott well in advance. We picked a Saturday, which was an active shopping day for locals and out-of-towners from the smaller surrounding counties. We went out on the streets with our boycott signs and leaflets. Many of the black patrons avoided the five- and ten-cent stores that we targeted. We did receive some verbal protest from a Negro woman shopper who criticized our efforts vehemently. We painfully recalled that the Benedict Arnold turned out to be an aunt of one of our strongest student movement members. When we look back at our accomplishments of that day, we try not to remember that incident. With our help, Mickey was able to step up his political activities. On Saturday, black people from the outlying counties would come into Meridian to do their shopping and would stop by the community center.

Freedom registration had been set up in Meridian, and we were able to reach some additional recruits from surrounding counties. Meridian was the next largest city for shoppers from Clarke, Neshoba, and Kemper Counties. As we walked the streets of Meridian with Mickey, we constantly heard insults, cursing, and racial slurs leveled at Mickey. Mickey was called "Jew boy" or "nigger lover." We weren't aware at the time, but we came to realize later that white thugs and police cars tailed him. He tried to hide it from us that he was picked up for questioning and received relentless threats. He seemed to downplay it and continued to operate with a sense of confidence and resolve that rubbed off on us. He didn't appear afraid, so we were not afraid. After one of our downtown protest marches, a number of us were arrested from the streets, taken to jail, and held in an undisclosed location. We were not able to make phone calls. When we didn't return to our rendezvous location, Mickey and J.E. realized that we had probably been arrested. We believe that some of the black cooks or matrons working in the jail got word out where we were being held. After dark, Mickey and J.E. located us from the outside of the jail. They were only able to see us through a small slit in one of the gated window visible from a side street. We had to reassure them that we were all right by revealing ourselves as they peeked through the window. We could see their heads and ears pressed closed to a partial opening as we listened to them whispering, "Are you guys Ok. How are you doing? Are you all right? We would parade ourselves one by one showing our faces so that they could see us. They continued this vigil until we were released.

Meridian

Meridian was known to be a "liberal" city in Mississippi—of course, that's a relative term. Black people were still expected to step off the sidewalk into the gutter when a white person walked by. The police were known as "burr-head busters," for their primary function was to "keep the poor folks out of the rich people's neighborhood." But the Meridian black community was proud that its thriving business district was not located across any set of railroad tracks but was instead an extension of the white downtown. The west end of Fifth Street made Meridian a well-known Mecca for black travelers in the Jim Crow South, offering two hotels, two restaurants, and a movie theater. Separate but equal seemed almost a reality in Meridian. After World War II, the expanding hair products market first put the Young's (one of our surrogates) in touch with black businessmen across the state. Young's beauty supplies were sold in black own pharmacies and beauty shops throughout Mississippi. Most prominent black businessmen in Mississippi knew one another and joined together in the state NAACP under the autocratic presidency of C. R. Darden, a Meridian photographer. Darden's part-time work as a salesman of high-school class rings enabled him to travel widely, performing his statewide responsibilities for the NAACP after completing his sales calls. Charles Darden was a strong proponent of voter registration and became targeted for retaliation. The picture window in the front of his home was repeatedly smashed and his class ring business boycotted. Forced to abandon many of his statewide political activities, he devoted more of his time to the local NAACP youth group. Both Charles Young and Albert Jones sat on a "biracial committee" composed of business and religious leaders of both races, who met regularly to discuss the city's problems. They introduced Matt Suarez (an early surrogate) to other members. Men like Charles Young, Albert Jones, and the Reverend Charles Johnson (NAACP Youth first contact) could provide Matt Suarez with a base of community support for the civil rights movement, but the actual workers had to be drawn among the city's black youth. Suarez's most valuable early contact was James E. Chaney (J.E) S. Brown and the three Sims: David, Marshall, and Bernice.

Born a Warrior, Just Seeking My Battle

By the time, I was fifteen, I, along with my two brothers, was active in the youth branch of the NAACP along with about nine others under the age of eighteen, to include James Chaney. We all had an enthusiasm for the movement that would mystify most of us today. My enthusiasm can probably be traced to three things: birth order, patriotism/political interest, and religious upbringing. It gave all of us a sense of belonging and doing something meaningful. It showed respect and was a political act in and of itself, breaking down barriers to caste and ending isolation, providing us with purpose and political activities. Black adults in Meridian and the surrounding counties, Suarez found, were terrified to be seen talking to a civil rights worker. Mass meetings, which could easily become known to the police, were out of the question. Despite Meridian's liberal reputation, black people in the area were as frightened as those in the Delta and rural areas. Building a movement of individuals willing to demonstrate the requisite courage to go down to the courthouse and register to vote was, as ever, going to be slow and painstaking work.

Throughout the last months of 1963, our little tight-knit group traveled to the nearby counties and surrounding areas of Meridian. James Chaney served as Matt's chief aide and driver most of the times. Some of the roads were dangerous after dark. Many times, we were able to accompany them on these "missions." Matt shared stories about the art of handling yourself if you got caught after dark and were confronted by the police or white knights. There was a code of behavior. Matt said that if you should ever be in a chase on the road at night, you put your accelerator to the floor and make a run for it. Under no circumstances were you to stop, especially for the police. Neshoba County, since the election of Sheriff Rainey and his appointment of Cecil Price as his deputy, appeared to be the most dangerous. Suarez knew about Rainey and Price from his days in Canton. Both officers had once lived in Madison County, and Rainey had been a Canton city policeman, serving as the constable of "Beat Five," where he began to cultivate a reputation as a law officer who was hard on blacks. Rainey's and Price's freewheeling style, their Western clothes and swagger, may well have been inspired by Billy Noble, the sheriff of Madison County, who not only wore Western garb and double six shooters but who also had been known to challenge local miscreants to meet him on the streets of downtown Canton for a Western-style "draw." In 1959, he shot and killed a black man visiting Philadelphia; the man was seated in a parked car with a former girlfriend. This black man was shot as he was attempting to comply with his orders. Rainey stated that he lurched at him in justification of the killing, and he was cleared of wrongdoing. There were no witnesses who would corroborate Rainey's testimony, but none would dare contradict it. (Rainey and Price, sheriff and deputy of Meridian, took part in the abduction and murder of Chaney, Goodman, and Schwerner.)

Blacks referred to him as "Mr. Cecil." Mr. Cecil had lost little time making certain the Neshoba blacks too learned to fear him. In a typical act of harassment, shortly after assuming the office of deputy sheriff, he rounded up a posse of Philadelphia city police one evening and led them on a raid of a roadhouse where young black people went to drink and dance. Striding onto the dance floor with his pistol drawn, Price announced a shakedown, mirthfully ordering the frightened patrons, "All you nigger men get your hands on the wall, and all you nigger wimmin do the dog." (Cagin & Dray: We are not Afraid).

One night while attending a school dance at our high school, we received a visit from the local police department. Two officers came into our gym and watched us as we danced. We had been told that there was a city ordinance that forbids us from doing one of the latest dances called *"the dog"*. If we were caught doing this dance, we could be arrested. As you can imagine, we felt very intimidated by this unusual visit at our school dance by the local police. We danced cautiously and respectful as they paraded among us on the dance floor. However, as soon as we were sure that they had driven off campus. Things changed drastically. I observed that even the most prim and proper girls from our school broke out in a raging rambunctious rendition of the dance never seen before. Perhaps, as a way to relieve that tension that we felt during those minutes that the formidable officers were scrutinizing us. I saw dance moves depicted that night which could easily compete with today's twerkers.

CHAPTER FIVE

Freedom Summer / MFDP (Mississippi Freedom Democratic Party)

Mississippi Freedom Summer Defined

Various authors use either "Summer Project" or "Freedom Summer" or both interchangeably. Summer Project refers specifically to the project organized and led by COFO (Council of Federated Organizations /SNCC (Student Non-Violent Coordinated Convention) and Freedom Summer to the totality of the movement's efforts in Mississippi over the summer of 1964.

Blacks had been denied the privilege of registering to vote by outrageous constraints and laws. A century after Reconstruction, pervading white fears of black political participation and control continued. Tactics for continuing disfranchisement of blacks were just a little less overt. There were other forms of intimidation to dissuade blacks from registering to vote: poll taxes, grandfather clauses, legal injustices, house burnings, job loss, house bombings, and threats of violence.

In order for the Mississippi Freedom vote to be successful, black citizens had to be able to write their names on this ballot. One of the goals of the freedom school was to teach literacy at least to the extent that illiterate blacks could write their names on a ballot that would signify that they could vote, providing the state of Mississippi's Jim Crow Laws removed some of the restrictions.

The Council of Federated Organizations (COFO), an umbrella organization of local and national civil rights groups founded in 1962, organized the Freedom Vote. The Freedom Vote had two main goals: to show Mississippi whites and the nation that blacks wanted to vote and to give blacks, many of whom had never voted, practice in casting a ballot. The mock vote pitted the actual candidates against candidates from the interracial Freedom Party.

Sixty white students from Yale and Stanford Universities came to Mississippi to help spread word of the Freedom Vote. Ninety-three thousand voted on the mock Election Day, and the Freedom Party candidates easily won.

After the success of the Freedom Vote, SNCC decided to send volunteers into Mississippi during the summer of 1964, a presidential election year, for a voter registration drives. It became known as Freedom Summer.

Bob Moses outlined the goals of Freedom Summer to prospective volunteers at Stanford University:

1. To expand black voter registration in the state
2. To organize a legally constituted "Freedom Democratic Party" that would challenge the whites-only Mississippi Democratic Party
3. To establish "freedom schools" to teach reading and math to black children
4. To open community centers where indigent blacks could obtain legal and medical assistance

Eight hundred students gathered for a weeklong orientation session at Western College for Women in Oxford, Ohio, that June. They were mostly white and young—the average age was twenty-one. They were also from well-to-do families, as the volunteers had to bring five hundred dollars for bail as well as money for living expenses, medical bills, and transportation home. SNCC's James Forman told them to be prepared for death. "I may be killed. You may be killed. The whole staff may go." He also told them to go quietly to jail if arrested, because "Mississippi is not the place to start conducting constitutional law classes for the policemen, many of whom don't have a fifth-grade education."

On June 21, 1964, the day after the first two hundred recruits left for Mississippi from Ohio, three workers, including one volunteer, disappeared. They had been taken to jail for trumped-up speeding charges and later released. At the beginning of the project in June 1964, these three workers—James Chaney, a Native Mississippian; Michael Schwerner from New York; and Andrew Goodman also from New York—were murdered in Neshoba County. While they were still missing, their bodies undiscovered, the

Mississippi Summer Project went into action. The deaths of the three civil rights volunteers became the cornerstone of the volunteers' movement. The Mississippi Freedom Summer began with the murder of Chaney, Schwerner, and Goodman and ended with the rejection of the Mississippi Freedom Party by 1964 Democrats. There were many suspicions that they would not be found alive. However, everyone involved continued the work of Freedom Summer. What happened next is not known. Local police were called when the men failed to perform a required check-in with Freedom Summer headquarters, but Sheriff Lawrence Rainey was convinced the men were hiding to gain publicity. Sheriff Rainey had built an ironclad alibi for himself the night of the murder. He made sure others saw him at the bedside of his wife at the hospital. The FBI did not get involved for a full day.

During the search for the missing workers, the FBI uncovered the bodies of three lynched blacks that had been missing for some time. The black community noted that their murders received nowhere near the same nationwide media attention that the murders of the three workers, two of whom were white, did. They had driven from Meridian to Longdale to inspect the ruins of Mount Zion Methodist Church (burned to the ground five days before. The congregation agreed that it could be used as a Freedom school for teaching young black children.

Freedom Schools

The freedom schools had a dual mission: to register as many blacks as possible to vote in the state of Mississippi and to bring black and white students as summer volunteers to work along with local groups. They established freedom schools, which introduced black history for the first time to many children as well as voter and citizenship education projects, informed local people of their rights to vote and federal programs available to them, and performed other tasks based upon the needs of the community where the workers were assigned. They also worked to unseat the regular Mississippi delegation at the Democratic Convention to be held in Atlantic City, New Jersey, in 1964. The founders of the movement had developed several means to accomplish this goal. Many blacks in the South were not able to attend school because they had to take care of the crops and cotton fields in order to survive. Many were not able to read or write. In order for the Mississippi freedom vote to be successful, black citizens had to be able to write their names on this ballot.

One of the goals of the freedom school was to teach literacy at least to the extent that illiterate blacks could write their names on a ballot that would signify that they could vote, providing the state of Mississippi removed some of the Jim Crow restrictions. Some of them were outrageous, including interpreting random articles from the state constitution (many learned scholars could not accomplish this), paying poll taxes imposed upon a people with little or no money, and the grandfather clause, which remained on the books. This clause declared that you could vote if your grandfather voted. Most grandfathers had been slaves and unable to vote. Added to these restrictions were threats of job loss and violence to body, home, property, and life and limb. Blacks had been denied the privilege of registering and voting by outrageous constraints and laws.

The freedom schools offered incentives to get people to sign up for the literacy classes—food, clothing, sewing fabric, books from the North, and a complete social community center for kids to play, socialize, and learn in a nonthreatening, nonjudgmental environment. I was glad to have a place to go after school. During my adolescence, I knew that there was a place for me. When my mother asked where was I going after school, the answer was: The Freedom School/Community Center. I felt connected to the school, cause, and the ideology. I was teaching people to read and write so that they could sign their names. Many blacks had to quit school in order to work in the cotton fields in order to survive. Schooling interfered with getting the crops ready in time for cultivation. I was more than happy to teach what I knew to older black citizens. Teaching them to read and write was rewarding enough for me. It was hardly a chore for what I would be getting out of it. Taking the literacy classes was a condition to get the books, fabrics, etc. My mother had taught both her male and female children the art of sewing. I was able to teach simple sewing techniques in the community. Freedom school coursework included creative writing, drama, art, journalism, and foreign languages and stressed the need for blacks to preserve their own culture rather than uncritically adopting white cultural values. Literacy, health, and typing existed in some community centers / freedom schools. Statewide, there were forty-one schools.

In our freedom school, we participated in drama classes and opportunities to do plays written by black authors and playwrights, like Leroy Jones and Lorraine Hansberry, and perform poetry by Langston Hughes, Zora Neal Thurston, etc. I remember in the freedom school performing Lorraine Hansberry's play *A Raisin in the Sun* for the entire student body and community. I played Mama and had to slap a fellow actor in the scene. The student actor I had to slap was not easy to get along with, and no one really liked her. Although I had wanted to slap her a hundred times, I still found it hard to slap my fellow thespian. I was learning songs in French and other languages, eating nourishing snacks, dancing, and communing with others like me. I was working with people who had been denied the rights of an education because of slavery. I gave out books to children. I worked in the COFO office performing numerous clerical tasks. In the Freedom School/Community center, I assisted seamstress department, taught literacy; gave out fabric to adults who agreed to attend literacy classes, and attended classes. In the field, I worked on voter's registration, and participated in protest marches and demonstrations.

The literacy component was the ultimate objective of the freedom schools. We talked about integrating the segregated swimming pools and equestrian camps to learn the art of horseback riding. I never got a chance to participate in these integration efforts; it was still too volatile and risky Pre-Freedom Summer. However, my younger siblings got a chance to participate a few years later. I missed the opportunities to swim in the integrated pools or picnic at Highland Park, or learn to ride a horse from the Meridian stables. My younger sister learned to ride and competed as a skillful equestrian.

There were so many resources available to us right there in Meridian, but we could not access them because of discrimination. We also learned that the federal government was funding all of these segregated facilities and that our hardworking parents were paying taxes to keep these facilities afloat, though we were not able to reap the benefits. These revelations only fueled my passion and commitment to fight, sing, march, and die if necessary to bring about a change. My dignity, life, liberty, and pursuit of happiness were being threatened. All those ideals spelled out in the Declaration of Independence that I believed in were being threatened.

After all, the United States went to war against Britain for these very same rights. These white Southern racists were now trying to prevent me from getting what was rightfully mine as a citizen of the United States of America. I knew where I was going and what I was doing after school.

As part of COFO efforts under the leadership of Rita, we obtain the freedom school, which was located only few blocks from my home on the same street. At one time, it had served as a kindergarten school called the Baptist Seminary. We held the statewide Freedom Summer Youth Convention in Meridian in August 1964. Our home, Meridian, was significant because we had the largest school in 1964.

In the rich history of the civil rights movement, the summer of 1964 stands out as one of its most significant periods.

It came to be known as Freedom Summer because it was during that time that COFO, a confederation of several civil rights organizations, brought nearly a thousand volunteers to Mississippi to work for civil rights. These mostly young volunteers worked on voter registration and community organization, and they operated freedom schools, the largest of which was in Meridian.

Seeing blacks and whites working, playing, and planning together for a common good, seeing all of the things that the white Southerners hated so much and said were not possible among the black and white races, was a kind of utopia that not only existed in my imagination; I saw it with my own eyes.

The Mississippi freedom ballot was a protest ballot signed by thousands of Negroes in the South in the early 1960s. It was the same ballot that set into motion efforts to unseat the all white Mississippi delegation in 1964 at the Democratic Convention in Atlantic City, NJ. It was at this convention that Fannie Lou Hamer pulled off her shirt and showed her scars from beatings that she had received from jailors while incarcerated as freedom worker and as a sharecropper in Ruleville, Mississippi. It was also at this Democratic National Convention that she delivered her "I Question America" speech.

The Mississippi Challenge

"I'll Be There" (Jackson 5)

On June 13, 1964, the first group of summer volunteers began training at Western College for Women in Oxford, Ohio.

Over three hundred college students participated in a week of orientation to prepare them to work on COFO voter registration projects. The following week, another group of volunteers attended orientation sessions to teach in freedom schools. COFO sought people who were realistic, responsible, flexible, and understanding. They had to pay for their own transportation, bond money in the event that they got arrested, and their food, lodging, and medical expenses. In the sixties, various civil rights groups working in Mississippi formed the Council of Federated organizations (COFO) and set the course of Freedom Summer. It changed Mississippi forever. The plan was to bring black and white students as summer volunteers to work along with local groups.

Freedom student volunteers came from middle- to upper-middle-class white homes in the North (Harvard, Stanford, Yale, Cornell, Mount Holyoke, Bryn Mawr, etc.). The staff people lived mostly in black Southern homes of lower-class parents. They came from SNCC (Student Nonviolence Coordinating Committee), CORE (Congress of Racial Equality), and sometimes from SCLC (Southern Christian Leadership Conference). The Freedom Summer volunteers were responding to a calling to come to the segregated South to advance efforts to end the disfranchisement of the Negroes. Adults were also instructed on how to go about registering to vote. They were there to provide the foundation for the freedom fighters that were being sent to test the waters of civil rights and to help end the overall disenfranchisement of the Negro in the South. It changed Mississippi forever.

In the months leading up to the convention, we were out in the field with our surrogate, Matt (Flukie), canvassing. We traveled tirelessly, seeking locations for voter registration sites: rural churches, country cafés, and homes. One evening, during one of our missions, we got caught out after dusk, which was the enemy in rural areas. Dusk seemed to come early in the rural South with no electricity. Backwoods roads after dark had degrees of darkness, which fell into the category of pitch-blackness. I remember that we sought shelter in an abandoned shack in a wooded area off the main roads because we thought the enemy (highway patrol) was in pursuit of us. Matt told us that the enemy was always looking for us, so we would hide whenever we were being pursued. In this abandoned house, we'd used a candle, which caused us to be spotted. We had a Molotov cocktail thrown through the open doorway, and about five of us jumped out of the back door into uncut weeds that reached well over ten feet. We dived blindly into the weeds. We avoided the engulfing flames. I had often wondered what a Molotov cocktail was. I learned that night that it wasn't something that you drank but something that you ran from. Whenever we saw this coke bottle flying through the air with a long white rag wick with liquid, we'd jumped. It made a noise when it hit something and created lots of fire. I was no longer ignorant as I lay in my weedy swimming pool.

Jackson, Mississippi: Precious Cargo

"Cuse Me, While I Kiss the Sky" (Jimmi Hendrix)

A crucial part of one of our missions with Flukie was to take the collected Freedom Ballots to Jackson, Mississippi, before the Democratic National Convention. Early volunteers had already begun these efforts before the official Summer Project convened as explained to us by our leader, Flukie. Freedom workers from all around the state were committed to this mandate: to collect as many freedom ballots as possible and take them to Jackson in order to be flown to Atlantic City, New Jersey. It was crucial that we get them there in time for a special plane scheduled to take them to New Jersey.

One evening, Matt stopped by the homes of about six members of our NAACP youth group. We were the ones trained and had been the most active with the organization. We had participated in collecting these freedom ballots along with him in many locations in Mississippi. Flukie had gotten permission from our parents for us to spend the night in Jackson, about ninety-three miles from our home in Meridian. He referred to Jackson as the rendezvous location. Flukie collected us from our homes with the approval of our parents as he had many times in the past. I was the second person to be picked up for this important trip to Jackson. When I reached his car, my taller female cousin was seated in the front seat with Flukie. As it turned out, Flukie was the only adult with us. There were many fieldworkers traveling that evening from several locations throughout mainly rural Mississippi. We picked up four additional members, who squeezed into the backseat. We would alternate sitting in the front to give the backseaters a break when we made nature stops. There were four of us in the backseat and three in the front.

To outsiders, we just looked like a typical black family, where often too many family members were sandwiched in one car. We had so looked forward to this event because most of our mission activities in the past were completed during the daytime hours and we were able to sleep in our own homes at night. But now, we would get a chance to sleep over in Jackson, our state capital. We would finally get a chance to sleep in one of the infamous freedom houses that we had heard so much about. We were so excited about the work that we had accomplished and understood the connection between our work and a much larger picture. We knew that these votes were going to change the landscape of our Mississippi world. They were protest ballots from black Mississippians that the world would hear about. We would get a chance to see many of the civil rights volunteers from other locations, which were doing some of the same work that we had been involved in. The only difference was they were older and we were still teens. It appeared that we had a special mission to reach Jackson where other civil rights workers had gathered. This was the evening that freedom votes were to be tallied and sent to New Jersey as Flukie related to our group.

All of the civil rights workers were coming together to count these special ballots. Much work, sweat, tears, and frustration had gone into getting these ballots. These freedom ballots had been collected throughout Mississippi. They were going to be tallied according to locations and labeled before being taken to Atlantic City, New Jersey. These were those precious votes that we collected from registered and unregistered black voters in the state before the official onset of Freedom Summer. This precious cargo containing these paper ballots represented the voice of all of those black people who had been silenced for so long—those black people who had weathered the storm and summoned up enough courage to place their names or that precious X on these ballots in the wake of all kinds of threats, real and imagined. These ballots would have an impact upon the delegations currently representing our state, as we understood it. This was a culmination of all of our efforts; this was the turning point to something really big. Tonight, we would get a chance to sleep over. We had joined the big girls' and boys' league. We were full team members in spite of our ages. All of the community work, literacy programs, and testy days that we spent getting doors shut in our faces resulted in good participation, and was not in vain. We had earned our place. The long walks in rural areas with no lights, endless days sitting through long sermons on hard benches just to get a chance to speak to pastors seems to be paying off. We had earned our place to be among the older volunteers who had come to Mississippi to set things right for us as a race. We had been working to gain the dignity and respect that we deserved as a people. We were fighting for our God-given rights to be free to vote, live, and have liberty and justice. Instinctively, we knew that this was bigger than all of us. We wanted to be a part of what we knew would change history forever. We were oblivious to the dangers, or we just didn't care. Liberty, justice, and freedom were worth all the mud-walking days and hiding out in the woods to elude the enemy lurking in the dark. We were not unlike Paul Revere sitting on the threshold of changing a nation.

The freedom ballots that we collected said in effect: "If I could vote, I would vote if not for the barriers you have placed upon me."

The freedom ballots were designed to unseat the regular Democratic delegation from Mississippi. They were set in place to effect change, and we had heard that white supremacists and the Klan knew of our activities. We knew that they were out to stop us any way that they could. We were told that they were especially on the lookout for us on this night in particular. They had our phone lines so they knew that this was a crucial stage of the movement. They also had their spies, and they had the electricity, gas, and water lines. They were on the lookout for us that night in particular at the culmination of the Mississippi Freedom Project.

I remember participating in a voter registration project that took me to the outskirts of the city limits of Meridian many times. On one of those occasions, we visited churches in rural areas where there was no electricity. Many times, we started out in the mornings trying to hit as many potential sites for voter registration campaigns as possible. We traveled tirelessly, seeking locations for future activities. The locations were mainly older rural churches, country cafés, and homes. We seemed always to be in a hurry to get as many voters as possible before the Democratic National Convention was to convene in Atlantic City, New Jersey, in 1964. We, the Mississippi Summer Project, had a mandate to fulfill, and the date was approaching fast.

We had to collect enough signatures on the freedom ballot in order to make a statement about blacks in the South who wanted to vote but couldn't. We had to collect enough signatures from blacks in Mississippi before the convention. The goal was to try to unseat the regular all white Mississippi delegates at the convention, showing a big number of "Freedom Ballots." (It was a congressional challenge: Mississippi's Freedom Democratic Party's efforts to remove five congressmen from their seats in the House). Sometimes, we would find ourselves leaving early and returning at dusk.

In many of these rural areas, there were poor lighting and no bold lights on the tall electric poles, which served some of the rural communities. We had driven all night dodging and eluding the highway patrol (which meant KKK to us). We learned to never trust any officer of the law because we knew most had white supremacist and Klan affiliation. Flukie know when to slow up and drive a moderate speed. We learned later that many were worried about us reaching our Jackson destination.

We had seen the highway patrol pass us several times, and we feared being stopped. On a few occasions, a highway patrol car would come past us, driving slowly and looking into our car. They would drive slowly and close enough that we could see their firearms on the backseat. Easily visible was long-gauge rifles and revolvers. Flukie drove slowly until they passed us on the highway. This happened a few times on our route to Jackson. We discovered that we were not stopped like many who were making this pilgrimage to Jackson. It appeared that our good fortune was related to our appearance as a family group rather than civil rights volunteers. Many of them traveled in pairs and integrated groups of blacks and whites. When this occurred, the white or black volunteer have to duck down low in the car to avoid being exposed. If they were seen riding together, this would serve as a dead giveaway that they were civil right volunteers.

Our travel arrangement gave the appearance of parent and five children squeezed into the backseat. Traveling in this fashion took place often in many poor families. My cousin was tall and she could past for an adult. The Klan usually knew of our activities and the whereabouts of the young-adult civil rights volunteers. They knew the cars and most of our activities, and our whereabouts, thanks to the cooperation of white public service workers in the telephone company and their relatives. Many volunteers borrowed local cars because they had been alerted. We knew that they were trying to stop us anyway they could. In those days, our offices depended a lot upon party telephone lines. It was too expensive to pay for a single phone lines. Racial slurs interrupted Many times our conversations and degrading messages. Even when we were able to acquire some individual phone lines, they still had their spies and monitored our movements. Our group was looking forward to getting to one of those freedom houses in Jackson to rest from what had been a long day. We were also curious because we had heard so much about them. Blacks and white freedom workers residing under one roof working together to effect change. There was an excitement that made us oblivious to the danger of being captured or lynched. We had no fear; there seemed to be only raw courage and power in unity.

We were entering a path to change history forever. We would be earning a voice, and not to be ignored or silenced any longer. I had heard so much about the Freedom houses, which received a lot of negative press by the southern media. Their locations were kept secret, and they constantly changed for safety. I was curious, however, about what went on in them with all of the negative press about the goings-on of whoremongering and miscegenation. I would get a chance to see with my own eyes one of these dens of iniquity—Satan's den of miscegenation. I was hopeful to finally get a chance to stay in one of these infamous houses. This opportunity would validate us as being on the same playing field as the adult volunteers.

Matt and our group finally arrived in Jackson after riding around for what seemed like all night to our weary souls. Although it was only ninety-three miles away from Meridian, it took us several hours to get there. I realized years later, that the roads that we took were not direct. Matt also selected many alternative routes as a way of escaping being seen by the highway patrol. The highway that exists today was not constructed in 1964. We started our quest to locate lodging in a freedom house for some weary travelers without much success. Matt drove to several freedom houses to seek lodging, however, they were filled to capacity. I got a chance to get out of the car, stretch my legs, and look around into several of them throughout the city of Jackson. Matt made several undisclosed stops, as he drove around in what appeared to be in circles throughout the city. I understand that they switched these private locations often for safety. I saw wonderful young people, black and white, from schools like Yale, Harvard, Columbia, and New York University working and playing together. Some seemed to be passing the time away playing cards; others were wrapped up in fetal positions in corners trying to catch a nap. Some were cautiously counting and recording the freedom ballots, organizing and wrapping them with such care and pride. Many were up at blackboards recording counties that had come in; leaving large space for UN recorded ones. Still there were others sitting at desks or talking on the phone, expressing hope that all the votes would get through in time. I understand that there was a special plane that had been chartered to fly those precious freedom votes to Atlantic City. There was a deadline we had to meet in order to be effective. I was not prepared for what it felt like. The feelings within me were almost indescribable. It looked as if I was in a dream state with my sleep lost delirium. We were so happy finally to see these houses and what was taking place. We had heard the negative rumors, but we didn't care. We would now officially be a part of the big league. We had finally made it. We had done our job with the freedom ballots, and now we would get our reward, a chance to sleep in the freedom houses.

We went throughout Jackson seeking space in one of the designated houses. So far, no room in the inn. Several homes had empty rooms with little or no furniture. Kerosene lamps provided some meager lighting, along with flashlights and camper's floodlights. Volunteers had their homemade backpacks or satchels to carry their meager belongings. They had to be able to move fast at any given time. Everyone seemed to know each other. There were expressions of joy that Flukie had somehow made it to Jackson. I was filled with joy as they rallied around us, laughing and hugging us. Little did I know at the time that many workers with freedom ballots in their cars were stopped by the highway patrol. The enemy knew that this was a key night to fly the ballots to New Jersey in time for the 1964 convention. We did not know that we had more than enough key ballots to meet the mandate with some to spare in our vehicle. He was carrying precious cargo—young teens and those precious protest votes that could make a difference now in our world.

Those ballots could change our lives after that night. They could change the world completely. We knew that things would never be the same after that night. After dropping off those ballots, we spent the remainder of the night looking for refuge. We continued our search to find a place for shelter, visiting several more freedom houses. We could relax, however, in the knowledge that the ballots had been delivered so close to the deadline. We were anxious that all of our efforts would not be in vain. Searching now for a place to sleep, Flukie appeared to drive in more circles, which we later discovered was a deliberate ruse. He finally stopped, and took the boxes of votes to a location that he kept secret from us. When we heard that we met the deadline, we were ecstatic, though exhausted.

What accounted for my delirium was my sleep deprivation because I don't recall even being up all night long without sleep. We passed many freedom houses that night, just how many we cannot recall. All I remember is that we had to pass them up, because there was not enough room. They all seemed packed wall to wall with sleeping people.

We were now approaching daylight. Finally, we pulled into the campus of Jackson State University. It was approximately 6:30 a.m. We pulled into the on-campus apartments near the girls' dorm. The only thing that mattered to us now was sleep. We quietly eased into a semi dark place, walked up a few stairs, and fell gratefully on the floor and sofa of a well-decorated large room. It was years later that I discovered our good slumber fortune was at the home of Dr. Margaret Walker, Professor and best selling Author of Jubilee. I finally went to sleep, but not without the nightmare of what could have happened to Flukie and six teenagers transporting precious cargo our "rendezvous" location.

Mississippi Freedom Democratic Party (MFDP) STANDS:

On August 22, MFDP presented its credentials, and the news media focused national attention on the group. Here were these "grassroots people" trying to upset the power of Mississippi. For more than seventy-five years, Mississippi had been permitted to perform it's, and the nation's business without a constitution ratified by its citizens. Who were these people who assumed that they could do the impossible? Fannie Lou Hamer was now known as "the former sharecropper" from the town of Ruleville in Sunflower County. She described, with clarity and great emotion, how she had been jailed. She left out nothing. The nation watched as she revealed body scars that she received from coerced black prisoners from her jailors and older scars from landowner when she sharecropped. The world saw this drama, and President Johnson hastily called a news conference to draw attention away from Mrs. Hamer and the parents of Chaney, Goodman, and Schwerner, who had come to lend support to the challenge. More delegates began to consider giving support to MFDP. For three days, the credentials committee was deadlocked on the issue. The president made it known that if the UAW and ADA wanted Senator Humphrey as his running mate for vice president; then they must use their forces to get MFDP to accept what he called an "at-large" status. At large usually means that delegates may be seated but may not represent the districts from which they were elected; they may represent the area, city, or state, as a whole but have no votes.

In reality, the MFDP was being offered "guest of the convention" status. They would represent no place at all and would not vote. The delegation refused the at-large status. Black leaders, in exchange for unity of the party, placed tremendous pressure so that Goldwater would not win the presidency. MFDP held out. They could not accept a position that left them out of all the proceedings. Various forms of intimidation were used to pressure them, which only caused them to get angry over tactics used. They began to get discouraged. "It's a token of rights on the back row that we get in Mississippi. We didn't come all this way for that mess again," said Mrs. Hamer.

They had come with faith in the system's fairness. They began to doubt what they had believed: that if the nation only knew what was happening in Mississippi, justice would prevail. They were offered an opportunity to participate in a grand ceremony, a march into the convention, with the eyes of the world upon them, and a chance to participate in a closed-door session alone. They emerged still believing that they had come to represent all those black people in Mississippi who had faced joblessness, starvation, and even death so that they could come to Atlantic City to cast their votes. They had not come merely to be seen or to be heard. They had come to participate. They had come to vote, to share in the hammering out of issues, and to have a voice in naming the standard-bearer of the Democratic Party. Being seated to represent Mississippi was their right. It was their responsibility to replace those who were illegally chosen and were being illegally accepted by that convention. Their answer was still *no*!

When the Mississippi Freedom Democrats arrived at the convention hall, all but three of the seats designated for the Mississippi delegation had been dismantled.

The sixty-eight members of the MFDP delegation stood where they felt they should have been seated. Those Mississippi blacks back home and other blacks across the nation who witnessed the scene will probably always remember that proud moment. They didn't achieve what they had come for. However, it did set the stage for a new day in the state of Mississippi. This was going to make a difference and lead to a change in the South. They believed that in taking this stand, they would be teaching older blacks who had never gone to school because they had to work in their own fields or sharecropping that they had been a part of something big, bigger than the ordinary. Once these black citizens were able to sign their own names, we would collect this freedom ballot. The collecting of these ballots and getting them recorded would gain the nation's attention—not just Mississippi's. We would be getting the nation's and the world's attention and bringing the focus upon the disparity brought on by the Jim Crows laws that denied a people the right to vote. All of these disenfranchised black people would have their voices heard finally at the 1964 Democratic Convention. These ballots would serve as a mirror to the world and show that in what was supposed to be a free nation, there had been some citizens of this country who had been disenfranchised, overlooked, rejected, and dejected for years, largely due to racism and discrimination set up under the rules of Jim Crow. They would be making a stand equivalent to Christopher Attucks, Paul Revere, and the soldier in the *Red Badge of Courage*. They would be saying to the world: "Look at all of these black people from Mississippi eligible to vote, but they have been left out of this wonderful system of government!"

Freedom Schools/Community Center:

The freedom schools offered many alternatives to our regular segregated school system; however, there was an underlying objective: to establish freedom ballots. The ultimate goal was to get enormous numbers of blacks in the South registered to vote. The freedom schools were just one vehicle by which they could teach literacy, so blacks would be able to sign their names on the freedom ballots, which said, in effect, "If you did not have these impossible restraints, I would be able to exercise my rights to vote. I am signing my name in protest that those elected to represent me are not my representatives because I did not vote for them. I never had the chance to exercise my freedom to vote. My signature represents the fact that I want my freedom to exercise my right to vote. Here is my freedom ballot, which I have affixed my name to. It was explained to me, and this is how I interpreted the freedom votes. You have had me in shackles. You have intimidated my family and me. You have even killed my ancestors. You made up impossible laws to keep me in bondage so I do not have any rights; you operate in a system that intimidates and humiliates me as a human being and attempts to treat me unlike a child of God. Here, I affix my signature even in an X. This X signifies that I have dignity, and by this X, I am exercising my freedom as a human being entitled to all the same liberties and entitlements granted to all citizens under the Constitution, but mainly under God."

The freedom ballot was a protest ballot signed by thousands of Negroes in the South in the early 1960s. Blacks had been denied the rights to register and vote by a number outrageous constraints and unfair Jim Crow laws: poll taxes, grandfather clauses, mandated interpretation of random selected passages from the Mississippi Constitution, and acts of violence carried out that destroyed home and life.

There were other forms of intimidation to dissuade blacks from registering to vote: legal injustices, house burnings, and threats of violence (house bombing, loss of jobs, physical abuse, and death). Many of the efforts leading to the MFDP and Democratic Convention in August 1964 took place after our comrades Mickey, Andy, and J.E. went missing. We went on, trying to continue our planned routine, with looming thoughts about their fate hanging in the air.

We were so proud to learn the freedom ballots that we worked so hard to obtain had set the stage for Ms. Fannie Lou Hamer's electrifying speech at the 1964 Democratic Convention. There was never any question that I would be going to the freedom school. It was a place that I could socialize; dine on healthy snacks, and most of all to allow my political consciousness to come alive. All those things that I was learning about in my history and government were being challenged and put to use every day. I could see the correlation between what I was learning about what this country was supposed to stand for, and see the discrepancies or inequities all at the same time. I was being fueled with energy to fight for a just cause, those rights ensured to all under our Constitution but, more importantly, under God.

We are all entitled to life, liberty, and the pursuit of happiness. I was so moved by the phrase "we hold these truths to be self-evident." I felt so connected to the school, cause, and ideology. I was also teaching people to read and write so that they could sign their names. I knew every day that I was doing a noble job. I understood why so many blacks in the South were illiterate.

They had to quit school in order to work in the cotton fields to survive. Schooling interfered with getting the crops ready in time for cultivation. The cotton had to be hoed, chopped, bagged, gathered, and weighed. I was working with people who had been denied the rights of an education because of slavery. I gave out books to children. I gave fabric to adults who agreed to attend literacy classes. I also taught simple sewing techniques in the freedom school. Attending literacy classes was a prerequisite to acquire the fabric and receive the books. It was such a good feeling every day knowing where I was going after school. I had a mission.

I understood the overall concept of this mission: we were teaching blacks to read and write their names as a protest and an exercise in freedom of speech all at the same time. We could see the connection of what we were doing in the freedom school and the impact upon the upcoming election. This was going to make a difference and lead to a change in the South. I just knew that I was a part of something big, bigger than the ordinary.

We helped brighten up the community center with paint, curtains, and bookshelves. Rita typed dozens of letters to friends and family up North, soliciting contributions of books, office supplies, and donations. By February, the community center was up and running and the first local black youngsters began to patronize it. The library boasted ten thousand volumes, donated by New York publishers to whom Rita had written, although at first there was not enough space to uncrate them all. No fines were levied on overdue books. Saturday afternoons, Mickey and Rita held a story hour for children between the ages of five and ten.

Transportation and refreshments were provided. In an effort to attract teenagers, a game room was set aside and equipped with a homemade Ping-Pong table and donated phonograph. Twice weekly, Mickey taught an evening class for adults in voter registration. Participants in all these activities were recruited by means of posters placed in nearby stores and restaurants and leaflets that Rita and Mickey Schwerner along with their initial recruits—James Chaney, Sue Brown, and the Sims—handed out on the streets, at church services, and at our basketball games at Harris High School. As we launched our outreach efforts during a basketball game, I took a few moments to observe Rita and Mickey interacting with these black students with such ease and confident. We'd never seen this kind of behavior between blacks and whites in Jim Crow south. They didn't seem uncomfortable at all as they were laughing and joking in this created integrated setting. Mickey knew sports and seemed to have gotten involved with the games and oblivious to how much he was being observed by these black kids during this rare sighting. I felt then that they had the winning combination to become part of this southern movement, which required integration of the races. We were distributing leaflets announcing what could be expected at the freedom school and community center. We knew that during these games that we could reach many student. There would be sewing classes, after school remedial tutoring in math and reading, arts and crafts, programs, and job training. Plans were underway to get a nurse to teach prenatal classes for expectant mothers and the establishment of a corps of volunteer carpenters who would go door-to-door in black neighborhoods and assist residents in making repairs to their dilapidated dwellings.

Mickey and the NAACP youth council had begun neighborhood canvassing in search of additional students for his voter registration classes. Matt had taken the first steps in the surrounding Newton, Kemper, and Clarke Counties. We were expanding from Lauderdale to other nearby counties. James Chaney and Michael Schwerner had begun to focus attention on the nearby rural county of Neshoba. Philadelphia, Mississippi only 37 miles from Meridian.

My Elementary School 4th - 6th

Freedom Summer Community Center/School
Old Baptist Seminary

Top photo: Author's Elementary School: Wechsler Elementary/
Bottom: Baptist Seminary served as Freedom School -Meridian, Ms. 1964

Harris High School

HARRIS High school

Harris High School

3photos of author's High School: Harris High School, 1964

Author, seated third from left. Statewide Freedom School Convention,
Registration Table. August 1964 Meridian, Ms.

Author's Sister: Rosemary Sims, Meridian Freedom School 1964.
Photo: Patti Miller, Freedom Summer Teacher

Photo by Donna Garde
Mark Levy Collection
Queens College/CUNY
Civil Rights Archive

Curious brother, Johnny R. Sims holding camera.
(Meridian Freedom School in 1964)

Author, standing 3rd from left, sister Artie Sims on right. Hospitality Table at Statewide Convention, August 1964.

Mark Levy Collection
Queens College/CUNY
Civil Rights Archive

Bob Moses: Speaking to Freedom Summer Workers

Meridian Freedom School Director with Students

Mark Levy Collection
Queens College/CUNY
Civil Rights Archive

Oxford, Ohio Freedom Summer Workers in-training. Summer, 1964

Fielder's Brook Bldg. COFO Office 2nd Floor. Meridian, Ms. 1964

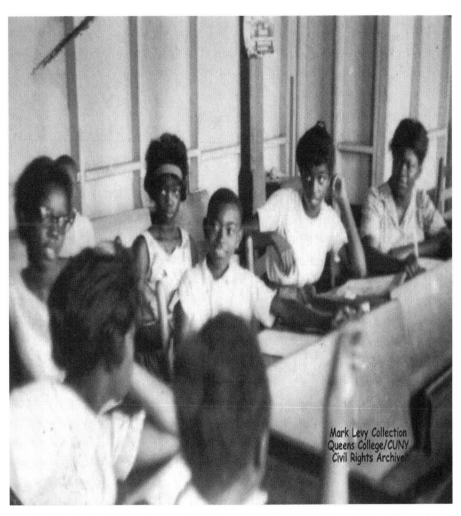

Author's brother, James E. Sims, third from left smiling. Five of author's siblings attended Freedom school. Meridian, Ms. 1964 (photos: Mark Levy)

Author's Brother, David Sims, Student Barber #1

Author w/Marshall, Student Barber #2

Jim Forman, (SNCC), Second left and A. Phillip Randolph, Right.

Photos by: Mark Levy and Donna Garde.

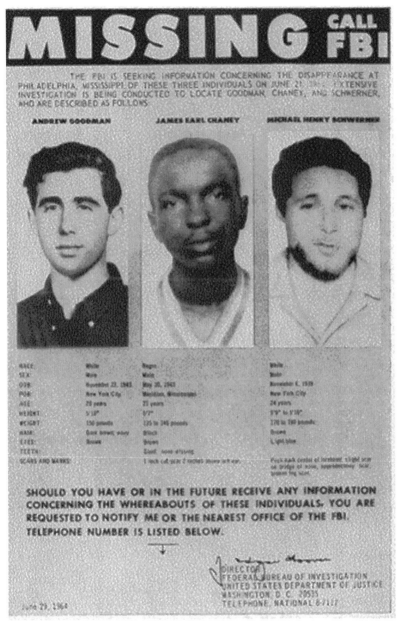

Missing Poster of the Three Martyrs

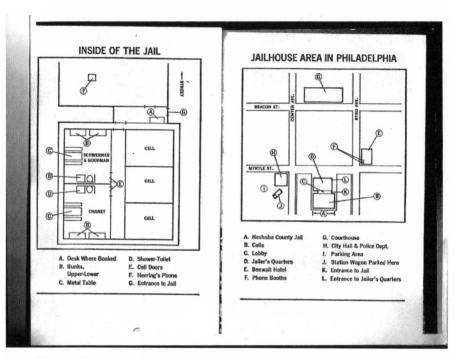

Photo of jail where Martyrs were held illegally, and location in Philadelphia, Ms.

Photo of charred civil rights vehicle located in Philadelphia, Ms.

Deputy Sheriff Cecil Price and Sheriff Lawrence Rainey at hearing in 1967 after arraignment. Convicted Conspirators in the murder of Chaney, Schwerner & Goodman.

Mark Levy Collection
Queens College/CUNY
Civil Rights Archive

Pete Seeger performing at Freedom School in Mississippi 1964.

Sister, Artie Sims third from left, Brother, Johnny, 4th from Left.

CHAPTER SIX

Sermon Before Midnight

"A Change is Gonna Come" (Sam Cooke)

Father's Day, June 21, 1964

It was Sunday morning, Father's Day at the Sims home. This particular Sunday started out like so many others around our house. Mother was making great strides toward getting us all up early to get ready for church. Father's Day, we knew, for the churchgoers would be an all-day affair. I was up and making a gigantic effort to help Mother in the kitchen, eyes still heavy with sleep but continuing to make extraordinary leaps and bounds to awake for the day. Let's face it; I am not a morning person—at least not back then. I was also contemplating a possible escape route from the long day of Sunday church services. I was hoping for some kind of reprieve. Sundays could be a trap if you had no other excuse-worthy plans. When I heard the civil rights vehicle roll into our dirt driveway and saw Mickey, I was hopeful. I smiled to myself because I envisioned that I might have gotten my wish after all. There was always something to do at the COFO office or community center, even on the weekends. It would be a welcome reprieve from listening to the minister preaching one of his long sermons honoring Father's Day. I looked out and saw my two friends and the new guy. We were accustomed to, and expected to see new people showing up all the time. We knew that freedom volunteers would be trickling in throughout the summer. I surmised that they were there to get one of my brothers who were not as busy to go with them on a mission. Maybe they needed another person. I had gone with them in past, especially to churches that we thought could serve as voter registration sites, or maybe go to the office to man the phones. They looked really tired and scraggly. It was my former next-door neighbor James Chaney (J.E.), who was now serving as a fieldworker, and Mickey, my buddy. I had come to know him pretty well now since meeting him and his wife, Rita over 6 months ago. They recruited me, my brothers, and a few other students from my high school to work with Freedom Summer.

James Chaney aka J.E., Michael Schwerner aka Mickey, and Andrew Goodman aka Andy came to my house to get haircuts and extend an invitation to my brothers David or Marshall to accompany them to Neshoba County. I asked to accompany them instead of my brothers, who had conflicting schedules. David had too many heads lined up to cut, and Marshall had just gotten his first car, which needed some work. Both brothers were good mechanics and barbers. Mickey and J.E. were also there to introduce us to the new recruit, Andrew Goodman, who wanted to be called Andy. They were en route to Neshoba County to investigate the charred remains of a church, which had been selected for a freedom school / community center site. Mickey wanted to let Andy know where he could get a cheap and professional haircut by either of my brothers. They wouldn't be able to go to our town to the white barbershops. Their Northern accents would be a giveaway, and they would be labeled and harassed as outside agitators. J.E. and Mickey wanted us also to get to know Andy, and help him to feel comfortable at our host home for freedom workers. Andy was also from New York, just like Mickey. He smiled often and appeared rather quiet. I thought that he was normally rather shy or probably taken in by the culture shock of being in Mississippi for the first time. He didn't come inside when he arrived as JE and Mickey had. In an effort to make him feel a little more comfortable, I went out to offer Andy some lunch and engage him in conversation. We discovered that we had some common interest. We both had an appreciation for the arts, theatre and government. We discussed the arts but focused most of our conversation on the role of government, the Constitution, and the Declaration of Independence, as he remained on our porch, (barber shop waiting room). The porch had chairs and the use of a bench that served as the waiting area for the patrons. You could tell that he was not as comfortable as J.E. and Mickey, who were almost permanent fixtures in my home. I was glad to take a break from the kitchen to go out and spend a little time with him. We both held strong views about what was lacking in this country's responsibility to be inclusive for all Americans. He told me that he had a younger brother about the same age as my brother, Johnny, who was about nine years of age. It seemed that the two of them had discovered each other and seemed to hit it off right away. He played with Johnny, while waiting on the porch. I peeked in and out to see them joking, tickling, and playing games like old pals. I noticed that he was demonstrating a craft game that we called making Jacob's ladder, using strings. You have to pull strings throughout your hand and fingers to make an edifice that resembles a ladder or a building. They seemed to be challenging each other with perfection and speed. Andy was showing him how to make this game using strings. I could hear them laughing and playing every time that I'd check on them. They would try to outdo each other with tricks that both seemed to be hiding up their sleeves. I think that my younger brother must have been fascinated that this young white man knew some of the same tricks that he knew. I could see that in a very short time, Andy would come into our home, get his haircut, and start reaching into the skillet to take out fried chicken or munching on cupcakes just like everyone else. It wouldn't take long; he would be an old-timer in no time at all. In the meantime, I took Andy seconds of cupcakes and fried chicken. I wondered if he wanted more but thought he was probably too shy to ask for it. I sensed that he needed more time to adjust. I did not want to infringe upon his sense of privacy. He seemed at peace with himself and his decision, whatever it was, and I did not want to appear pushy. We talked some, but I noticed that he really seemed to enjoy playing with my younger brother Johnny. Andy shared that he was looking forward to speaking with his brother and father later on that day.

I left them alone to go check on the new batch of cupcakes and fried chicken that my mom was making to send with them as a snack for their trip to Neshoba County.

They told us that they had met and recruited Andy from the Freedom Summer training site in Ohio. Andy was initially assigned to another location in Mississippi; however, a decision was reached that he would be a perfect personality match to work with Mickey and J.E. They were among the first group to receive training in preparation for freedom summer. This was a planned project by SNCC and other coordinated civil rights organizations made up mainly of northern college students. They were responding to a calling to come to the segregated South to increase voter registration in the Negro communities. They were there to lay the foundation for the freedom volunteers being sent to test the waters of civil rights, and help to remove barriers that have been disenfranchising Negroes in the South. We had initially heard about this movement coming to Mississippi over a year ago through our NAACP youth involvement. Mickey and Rita had thoroughly explained to us about the goals of Freedom Summer a few months earlier. We would be seeing more recruits come down to Meridian to work in the community center, freedom school, and canvassing toward increasing voter registrations.

I could always figure out how to juggle my chores with Mother in the kitchen and finding out about movement plans with my colleagues. Mickey, J.E., my brothers, and I were always interested in the latest goings-on and how we would fit into upcoming plans. There were always many things to be done, and by now, I was just another soldier waiting for duty. Listening and checking on Mom in the kitchen, I told her about our new morning guest, and she ushered me to return to the kitchen to help her. We were preparing food for the home as well. The kind of foods that had a longer shelf life for our full day ahead. You could never go wrong with fried chicken, cupcakes, and macaroni and cheese. They were popular staples in many southern African-American families. These delicacies were easy to transport and popular for their extended shelf life without refrigeration. Going to church on any Sunday in the South meant long hours. We were expected to attend Sunday school in the morning, regular afternoon worship services, BTU (Baptist Training Union at 5:00 p.m., and evening service, which started at 7:00 p.m. If we got a break, it might be somewhere between regular worship service and BTU. Mother wanted to make sure we had prepared enough food for them, as she heard that they would be leaving from our home to go on a planned field mission site near Philadelphia. We had heard about the troubles with the church people who were beaten by a white mob the week before, and the burning of the church. This site had been selected to be used as a Freedom School and community center similar to ours in Meridian. J.E. would be doing the driving, and he mentioned that they were off scheduled based upon the written plans left at the COFO office with a staff member.

The sound of our radio was playing in the background along with the buzzing sound of the electric clippers. Church music and old time spirituals could be heard over the radio that was setting the stage for the minister's sermon. According to my mother, he was a good preacher, and this was going to be a good message. This old Baptist radio minister could now be heard clearing his throat, getting ready to preach one of his hellfire-and-damnation-for sinner's sermons, warning us about the dangers of not repenting. His plea was for all sinners to make the commitment to follow Christ as the only means to salvation. The sermon was supplemented with richly voiced gospel singing. Our Father's Day morning was emanating Sunday morning blessings as a prelude to more to come.

The smells of coffee, fried bacon, chicken, and baked macaroni was coming from Mama's kitchen. All these smells emanating from the kitchen meant Sunday morning had arrived. If I needed further proof, it would be the uplifting sounds of Mother humming to the gospel music echoing in the background. I could see her now beginning to hum in that satisfying tone. Yes, Sunday morning had arrived whether I wanted it or not. Mickey and J.E. came into the kitchen as usual. Mickey and my mom had their usual love fest where they argued about religion as he ate whatever she was cooking in the kitchen.

The kitchen was their usual spot to solve all religious and worldly problems. We thought that Mickey sometimes tested our mother about being agnostic, which she had a hard time accepting. He told us that he believed in the goodness of man. She also had found it hard to believe that everyone did not accept Jesus Christ as his or her personal savior. The concept of being Jewish and still waiting for the Messiah was a huge leap for her Christian understanding. She came to the conclusion that Mickey was really an atheist, and just needed to be led in the right direction. In time, she was confident that he would accept the Lord, Jesus Christ. Being an agnostic was not a concept that she could easily digest. Every time the two of them got together, they argued about religion. Both Mickey and mother remained unmoved in their belief systems and argued continually. When J.E. saw them about to get started, he just smiled and left the kitchen. Mickey and mother argued often while he enjoyed her Southern cooking. We had learned to respect this as their bonding time together, and would also just leave them alone. We thought of this as a kind of "love fest" because it was friendly and never mean-spirited. Both seemed to enjoy this time that they spent together.

My brothers, David and Marshall (the barbers) were up early too in preparation to receive the churchgoing and non-churchgoing patrons coming in for haircuts at the makeship barbershop. The churchgoing customers came by early on Saturday or Sunday to be first in line, so that they could avoid the rush that was sure to come. My brothers had so many heads already lined up to cut before 9:00 a.m., thereby giving them a pass from church attendance that day. They usually only cut hair on weekends when they were not involved in movement work. Our makeshift barbershop was situated on the right side of our porch. The barbershop was equipped with wooden chairs, a bench, and wooden rattan shutters. The loosely fitted wooden shutters provided just the right amount of light and comfort. There were also shade trees from our neighbor's yard, which provided some privacy. James Chaney, a.k.a. J.E. lived next door to the right of our home for years. His family had recently moved to a new home just a few blocks away. Mickey and J.E. had been permanent fixtures at our home, and they were fully aware of my brother's weekend routine and the volume of work ahead of them.

Word got around quickly that my brothers were good at cutting all hair types. David became the barber for many of the female freedom workers. He gave them easily managed short haircuts and sassy bobs. Some of the volunteers had begun to trickle down early to get an early start on their Freedom Summer work assignments. I helped out by keeping their makeshift barbershop clean and orderly, sterilizing combs and scissors and constantly sweeping and picking up the cut hair from the floor. I kept things as clean and neat as possible. My mother insisted upon the constant cleaning of the assigned barbershop area in our home. We were fortunate that my older sister worked in an established hair salon on Fifth Street. She was able to acquire those large vessels of blue sterilizing liquids and other supplies. All of the newly arriving white freedom workers (male and female) knew that they could get a professional haircut by my brothers. My home would be become known as the barbershop for the Freedom Summer workers. My brothers' hair-cutting skills were well known throughout the community as well. It did not take long before this news had spread among all the newly recruited freedom workers who had been assigned to Meridian. My mother had trained my brother to give professional haircuts to both blacks and whites. My mother was a naturally talented person in so many areas. It is hard to say where she obtained the knowledge. She had the ability to observe a process for a short time and just master it. My brothers (David and Marshall) were often referred to as "student barbers" because they were still attending school while working in the Mississippi movement, which included Meridian, Lauderdale, and other surrounding counties.

The trio told us that they had driven all night from the Women's College in Oxford, Ohio, where their training took place. They left Ohio Saturday, June 20 at about 3:00 a.m. and reached Meridian that night close to 8:30 p.m. They really looked tired and scraggly and admitted that they had driven all night on Saturday without stopping as they got closer to Mississippi. They thought it would be too risky to stop, so they drove all night. They said that by driving at night, they would be less conspicuous. White and black workers traveling together stood out like a sore thumb during the day, but at night, they could avoid a lot of scrutiny. They talked about how they took turns driving and hiding out in the backseat, especially if they thought that they would be recognized.

They shared with us stories about the non-violent tactics and other student that they had met who were coming down to Mississippi for the summer. Andy enjoyed drama, and during the training, they performed role-playing to illustrate the various kinds of intimidations that they could be subjected to by white jailers if arrested. Andy played the role of the enemy abusive jailer intimidating the civil rights volunteers.

Just a few days earlier, we had heard stories of how they had firebombed a black church in the county and had beaten terrified worshipers. Some of them required hospitalization. Members of an angry white supremacist mob disrupted the church service and were demanding to know the whereabouts of "goatee". This was the code name for Mickey given by the KKK because he had sported this type of beard (goatee).

Mickey and J.E. were aware of the disruption, but this did not seem to deter them from wanting to make this trip. Knowing Mickey as we did, I am sure that he probably felt that he needed to see about some of the volunteers who had been hospitalized. He was concerned about the people who had been hurt, and wanted to offer them some support. We thought that he might have felt responsible because they had agreed to cooperate with the movement. Mickey and J.E. had spent several weeks up there putting things in motion. That morning, we talked about the danger, especially now that the Civil Rights Act had just passed. In many of the southern newspapers, they were full of accounts about the volunteers coming to Mississippi, and being referred to as the enemy. Southern defiant whites called it: "The Summer Invasion".

My mother heard about what had happened to the church people the week before. She asked Mickey if it wouldn't be better to let things die down some before going up there. She told them that the hate seemed to have gotten worst over the past weeks. She tried to entice him to wait until one of her famous pies came out of the oven. Mother wanted the trio to stay long enough to have an early sit down lunch. We knew that this was her way of just trying to get them to delay the mission. They said that they had eaten breakfast at the café downtown earlier, and planned to return to Meridian from Philadelphia by 4:00PM. Both David and Marshall declined their invitation to go to Neshoba County with them because both had a full schedule. David had asked if they could alter their schedule, and pick him up a little later. Mickey told him that they were already late based upon their written schedule left at the COFO office.

J.E. said, "Man, you had better go with us." I want my freedom, and I want it now. I am tired of waiting." He had also begun to lament a lot about his "baby girl." One got the impression that he had seen her that morning or before he left for Ohio. I recalled him saying, "I just saw my daughter, and I am doing this for her. He continued to say, "Man, I am doing this for my daughter." He smiled often as he talked about his "baby girl." He told me, "I went by and saw my baby girl." It is not known the exact time that he went by to see her. From my observations, the thought of her really made him happy. He also seemed to tie in what he was doing in the struggle as a way of making life better for his daughter. He said often, "I'm doing this for her." He kept saying, "I want my freedom now, and I don't want my daughter to go through what we are going through now. I want to do all that I can to make this world a better place for my daughter."

J.E. was also teasing me in his usual way. He seemed to know about my cache of wealth that I had hidden somewhere. I was always holding out on him and the rest of the world. He knew about wealth that I was not aware of. He would always start with a hello in that slow, soft voice and that easy warm smile of his to try to wear me down, I guess.

After that infectious smile of his, He'd ask me to give him a dollar, only a dollar; it would always be just a dollar. I thought just to bug me. My respond would always be the same:

"J.E., now, you know that I don't have any money." He always asked, and my reply was always the same. I often wondered why would he keep asking me for the same thing, when he knew my answer was always the same.

Sometimes, I thought that he just didn't hear me as he laughed and smiled at my answer, especially when I seemed so serious or appeared to be annoyed. I later came to realize that he just loved having fun with me; there was nothing wrong with his hearing.

They told my brothers that they were trying to stay as close as possible to their schedule and would not be able to return to get them later. Mickey said that they had made plans to return to Meridian before dark. I also wanted to go and suggested that I could replace one of my brothers on this trip. I saw a real opportunity to escape from the long day's Sunday church services. Mickey and I began to argue. He was adamant in his refusal to let me go on this trip. I protested a lot; however, I lost the male chauvinism argument. Mickey told me that they were going to be looking over the remains of a burned site that was to be used for voter registration. He rejected my request and said that it wouldn't be an appropriate place for a girl in a dress. He said that there would be a lot of burned rubbish to be stepping over, and it could prove dangerous for females. I eventually lost the argument when he told me that my services would be needed more at the COFO office. He convinced me that there was a greater need for me to help man the COFO office phones in Meridian. Working in the office, and taking telephone calls was a normal occurrence for me, especially when workers were out in the field. There was always a need for someone to be in the office to receive those infamous 4:00

p.m. call. The 4:00 p.m. call informed everyone concerned that the planned field activities had gone as expected. If he talked about the need for my help in terms of what was best for the overall movement, then that usually settled me down. Somehow, I knew that what we were doing in those early days in the freedom movement was larger than what we were doing on the surface. I always felt that it was connected to a superior purpose, and my momentary whims didn't matter as much as the bigger picture. It somehow rang sacred in movement language for me.

After Mickey got his hair cut, he went out back to offer assistance to my younger sibling in beating the older ones in a game of "fair" basketball. Mickey had a strong sense of fairness, so he would not hesitate to give the challenged an "unfair" advantage. We had a makeshift basketball court complete with net and backboard in the backyard. Mickey was always looking out for the younger ones or ones he felt were disadvantaged and would find ways to give them an edge. He would pick my six-year-old sister up in the air and carry her on his shoulders to shoot the basketball through the hoop.

He would laugh so hard that his belly shook when the older kids complained that this was unfair and accused him of cheating. Subsequently, Mickey made his way back into the house and to Mama Sims's kitchen. The backyard was the closest to the kitchen. On this particular morning, Mama Sims had posted a newspaper clipping on the wall above our dining room table. On the front page of our local newspaper, the Meridian Star was a caption that stopped Mickey cold in his tracks. He found it puzzling and funny at the same time. The caption read: "Crime does not Pay." Underneath the caption was a photograph of a man pinned under a car. It appeared that a thief was attempting to disable a car to steal parts. The car collapsed on him, pinning him to the ground, and he was crushed to death for his efforts. Mickey found it incredulous and belly-laughing funny that our mom had pasted this newspaper clipping above our breakfast table. He asked, "But why over the eating table?" I told him that I guessed she wanted to make sure that we really didn't miss seeing this newspaper article and photo. I told him that she had a special way of reinforcing our understanding of moral lessons. He just couldn't help himself from laughing about the way in which my mother reinforced moral lessons to us concerning stealing. He became so overcome with laughter and seemingly couldn't help himself, and before long, it became infectious. We all started laughing. J.E., Andy, and my brothers—everybody was laughing except my mother. She didn't understand what we thought was so funny. She remarked, "You are all too silly." My mother was that way; she had a very dry sense of humor and would say the funniest things, but she never understood her own humor, which made things even funnier.

Every time Mickey would draw a breath, he would ask, "But why, why, why over the table?" I tried to answer in my own way; I was so accustomed to Mother being so demonstrative when she wanted to get a point across. It was kind of hard to explain this to someone else. I also told him about the times that she would make us hug each other after fighting and wouldn't allow us to release from each other until she was satisfied that we were no longer angry with each other. We could avoid laughter as long as we didn't have to look each other in the eye. After a while, Mother would force us to look at each other face-to-face, and that would usually end our anger toward each other. We would end up breaking up into belly-wrenching laughter.

It was Andy's turn to get his hair cut by my brother David. He had cut Mickey's hair first. We felt that this was done partially to give Andy a chance to see how skillful my brother were in cutting white people's hair. I'll go first, and you can see his work, was probably his thinking. It also gave Mickey a chance to spend more time in the kitchen with his pal. Mother and Mickey were again in the kitchen together, and almost on cue, they began their ongoing argument about religion. Mickey was eating whatever was ready or resting from the stove. He enjoyed leftovers, and especially liked the crusty toasted parts around the edges of the baked macaroni casserole. What we thought was overcooked or slightly burned part; he revealed that this was his favorite. The love between them was obvious to everyone around, and we usually disappeared to let them enjoy quality time. My mother would often comment on how we wasted so much food, and Mickey ate well. He was a bite chubby around the middle, and to my Mom, that meant that he was healthy.

We all recognized this was an integral part of their normal ritual. On this morning, like so many others, Mickey reminded my mother that he was Jewish and not a Christian. He told her that he didn't disbelieve in God; however, he was agnostic and believed in the "goodness of man." He often said, "When tested, ultimately, man would prevail victoriously and would do good over evil." Since my mother never really comprehended his Judaism, and waiting on a Messiah, she just set her sights on converting Mickey, the atheist, to Christianity. The radio was still blaring with the minister preaching his Sunday morning sermon. They both began to listen. The tempo and pitch of the Baptist minister changed to a more fervent, energetic one. Mickey joined in with the radio preacher's sermon. He began mimicking to sanction back to the preacher with perfect pitch and a timely call and response. He started clearing his vocal cords and adopted a tenor close to the preacher's. He repeated quotations from the radio preacher while making up some of his own. He sang songs of salvation that I had never heard before. Andy came in from the porch and began to join in after following our lead for a while. I saw him smiling as he joined us in song. Many of the songs' lyrics repeated themselves, so it was easy to fall into the cadence of the singing. J.E. was laughing and singing as well. We all had begun to listen to the going ons from the kitchen. Mickey just seem to take off and began his own soliloquy about "getting things right" before it was too late, which was echoed by my mother singing, "You better get it right before it is too late." There was humming and singing at various points, and the rest of us began to join in the fun, impromptu but timely. Mickey continued on a fervent pitch and began with exaltations of "Yeah, yeah, yeah, amen, amen, amen, umhuh, huh, umhuhh, yeah, amen, preach! Roll on, dear brothers and sisters, on and on." His timing was so well orchestrated that it took on a fervent pitch and voice all of its own. After a while, it became confusing to all of us. We were no longer laughing or smiling. Were we playing, was this an act? After a while, no one was laughing anymore, nor was Mickey or my mother. My mother never laughed as she always maintained a serious tone and demeanor throughout Mickey's soliloquy. What was happening? Everyone seemed to have fallen into a familiar place or just respecting what we were taught upon hearing the spiritual words by whoever was delivering them. It was very natural for my family and me to respect all religious efforts. She joined him in song and praise, and we followed.

My father, who had a rich gospel voice, began to sing one of his old tunes of "give me that ole time religion; it is good enough for me." He led us with

"This little light of mine, I'm going to let it shine." We joined in to chorus with my father's lead. My father and Mickey would share in the lead. Mickey was in full swing into his Baptist minister soliloquy, preaching and humming and singing very convincingly to all who were listening. Mother was smiling ear to ear and began to sing, "Take my hand, precious Lord. Lead me on. I'm so glad that Jesus lifted me." Mickey began to sing with her, and we all got caught up in this spiritual frenzy of Mickey's preaching, praising, and singing. I never knew Mickey was so familiar with some of these Negro spirituals. After some time, his "sermon" just didn't seem funny anymore. We were brought up to respect traditional religious customs, and if someone were making an effort, we'd demonstrate respect and reverence. Andy and J.E. began to fall into our assumed religious community, which had been set into motion. Andy and J.E. egged him on as well with amen's and praises to the Lord while humming in deep harmony with my dad. I had never heard J.E. sing before. He echoed sounds from voices of seasoned deacons from the mourning bench. After a while, my father protested, "I just don't want to leave. I just don't want to leave for work right now. I feel like I'm in church. Looks like I won't have to miss church after all." He was constantly giving prompts of call and response to support Mickey's sermon: "Yeah, Yeah, Yeah, Amen and hallelujah, Praise the Lord, Thank You heavenly Father, Amen". It lasted for a while, we were all so wrapped up that it is hard to say how long it lasted. Where did the joking, teasing, or pulling of my mother's leg , or did something else happen? I don't think that we will ever really know. Mickey sounded so authentic, and his responses were right on. There was such a serene look upon his face, and no one was laughing anymore. Mickey's voice began to take on a different cadence and fervor, which demanded this kind of respect. It appeared that he had removed himself from us emotionally and remained in this spiritual frame of mind. He didn't seem self-conscious or apologetic, and this helped us to pay attention to him. The only person who seemed to have a confident smile of reverence on her face was my mother. She wasn't confused or puzzled as we had been earlier. I guess that she felt that the moment had finally arrived. Mickey had accepted Christ as his personal savior. She had hoped and prayed for this day to come, and it was today. "Praise the Lord!" She also received some satisfaction that she had won her religious battle with Mickey. Finally, it had happened after all of those months of arguing with him. You could not tell her that Mickey did not become a Christian and come to accept Jesus Christ as his personal savior that morning.

My father was up in full spirit as he was in preparation for the afternoon work shift. He had been sleeping but was led to the room where Mickey was preaching in a perfect pitch that overpowered the Baptist radio minister. My dad said, "Now I don't have to miss church after all."

I am sure that my mother finally got her wish. I am sure that she thought that she had brought her Jewish son to salvation. Years later, when she finally accepted their deaths, she commented upon that last day with them. She said that she received some comfort in knowing that they went to heaven. She knew that Mickey finally accepted Christ before he died. She found relief and some solace in the fact that she knew Mickey was saved that morning. Salvation had finally come to her Jewish son.

It was now time to leave, and Mickey only had a twenty-dollar bill to pay for the haircut. I was selected to go to the store to make change. I returned with $19.50. (The FBI reports said that they were arrested for speeding in Philadelphia and were unable to pay the twenty-dollar speeding ticket.) Mickey had given me permission to buy myself something for my efforts. Upon hearing about the trouble the week before, my mother tried to get them to wait until some of the bad feelings began to die down. She shared that she was very anxious about them going up there. She tried to entice them to delay by trying to get them to sit down and eat. They appeased her by agreeing to take some lunch. I had packed some extra fried chicken and cupcakes in a brown paper bag for their journey to Philadelphia. When I reached the front door, the car had taken off down Thirty-First Avenue. I chased after the station wagon, running in the middle of the street, hoping that they would stop and see me in their rearview mirror. I watched the station wagon as it turned the corner before I could reach them. I stood in the street for a few minutes waving these two brown bags with their greasy spots.

CHAPTER SEVEN

Murder/Conspiracy/Justice

Early Family Memories of Philadelphia, Mississippi

I recall on several occasions, my siblings and I would accompany Dad on his periodic visits to Philadelphia, Mississippi. It was a small rural town approximately thirty-five miles away. It had the only existing gristmill that grinds corn to make fresh cornmeal. We continued to use the gristmill until it closed down. Although, it was less than an hour drive by car, it seemed like hours to five -year-old.

Taking that car ride to Philadelphia always made me feel uncomfortable, and I never really enjoyed the trip. I don't know why, but it seemed that each time that we took the trip, it was usually raining. The place always looked spooky behind the dark clouds of billowing smoke emanating from the distant mill.

You could see the dark smoke before the mill was visible. I knew that I always felt better when we were returning home. Philadelphia had a large community of Native Americans. I never enjoyed looking at them, mainly because at that time, I did not have an appreciation of my own Native American roots. It was uncomfortable looking at their rather distant, distraught, and anguished faces. They seemed to be moving aimlessly throughout a community that only tolerated them. This same town would later provide us with a more realistic and painful memory when the KKK murdered my colleagues, James Chaney, Michael Schwerner, and Andrew Goodman.

Philadelphia's History: (Seth Cagin/Phil Dray:" We Are Not Afraid")

"The county was Philadelphia was located in what was to become known as Bloody Neshoba (The County of Philadelphia Miss).

During the Depression, a Bonnie and Clyde–style gangster named Charlie Chapman briefly terrorized the area. A Philadelphia road contractor, his business went under, and a bank repossessed everything he owned. To retaliate, he became a bank robber, and he enjoyed a prolific career in Neshoba, Winston, Kemper, Newton, and surrounding counties before being ambushed and shot to death on Highway 16 east of Philadelphia. His bullet-ridden corpse was placed on public display in Meridian.

There were never many blacks in Neshoba County. A 1920 census found 15,872 whites, 2,929 Negroes, and 477 Choctaws. By 1964, blacks still amounted to about 15 percent of the total country population of twenty thousand with Choctaws having grown to form another 15 percent.

The railroad tracks of the Gulf, Mobile, and Ohio separated white Philadelphia from Independence Quarters, the black shantytown that stood to the west of town.

Water and electric services there were dismal. Few homes had indoor plumbing. The neighborhood streets were rutted and unpaved, and the US Post Office did not serve residents with home delivery. Here, as in most Mississippi towns, "the other side of the tracks" bespoke another universe.

Philadelphia residents were so accustomed to racial inequities that many were surprised when, after the disappearance of Goodman, Schwerner, and Chaney, a *New York Times* reporter described the Negro section of Philadelphia as beginning "where the sidewalks and pavement end." But when they looked, they found that what he had written was true. Similarly, Philadelphia whites, like whites elsewhere, were blind to black resentment and discontent. Even the most progressive whites expressed a casually paternalistic attitude toward blacks. Chaney, Schwerner, and Goodman were arrested and released at night without being able to telephone anyone. The Justice Department was informed, but the FBI did not enter the case for more than a day. Their disappearance immediately focused national attention on the Summer Project. The incident did not result in basic changes in federal policy regarding the protection of civil rights workers. President Johnson authorized the use of two hundred navy sailors in the search for the missing workers and at least 150 FBI agents. Former CIA director, Allan Dulles and FBI Director J. Edgar Hoover visited the state to coordinate the new federal involvement.

On August 4, 1964, the three bodies were found in an earth-fill dam near Philadelphia, Mississippi. My fiancé was a member of the navy search party who discovered their bodies.

Sunday, June 21, 1964, three young civil rights workers—twenty-one-year-old black Mississippian James Chaney and two white New Yorkers, Andrew Goodman, twenty, and Michael Schwerner, twenty-four—were murdered near Philadelphia, in Neshoba County, Mississippi. They had been working to register black voters in Mississippi during Freedom Summer and had gone to investigate the burning of a black church.

The Neshoba County Police held them for several hours and later released them after dark into the hands of the Ku Klux Klan, who beat and murdered them. They were arrested and released at night without being able to telephone anyone. After the three were arrested and released from jail, they had a flat tire. They we were ordered to repair the flat tire. Mickey was sitting in the sheriff's patrol car in Neshoba County before their abduction. He picked up the sheriff's revolver that he'd dropped from the seat and handed it to him.

At one point, Mickey handed Patrolman Poe (the arresting officer in Neshoba County) his gun, a Magnum .357. In the warm weather, he often took it off and let it remain on the seat.

It was later proven in court that a conspiracy existed between members of Neshoba County's law enforcement and the Ku Klux Klan to kill them.

According to FBI reports, "The murder took place near Philadelphia, Ms. at the end of a road called: Rock Cut Road. The location is about a mile from where the three men were taken from the station wagon widely recognized as the civil rights vehicle. The murder took place before Midnight, and the moon was still high. It is reported that three of the victims said nothing. But that they were jeered by the murderers. Several of the murderers chanted in unison: 'Ashes to ashes, Dust to dust, if you'd stayed where you belonged, you wouldn't be here with us.' Another said: 'So you wanted to come to Mississippi? Well, now we're gonna let you stay here with us.'" ("Three Lives for Miss: By William Bradford Huie"/FBI Report: MiBurn-Mississippi Burning Case Testimony).

When Schwerner was pulled from the car and stood up to be shot, it was reported that the man with the pistol asked him, "You still think a nigger's as good as I am?" No time to reply, he was shot straight through the heart and fell to the ground. Goodman was next, with nothing said. He stood as still as Schwerner did, facing his executioner, for the shot that killed him was the same precise shot. Chaney was last, and the only difference was that he struggled while the others had not. He didn't stand still; he tried to pull and duck away from his executioner. He was shot three times. It is told that Chaney recognized one of the men from Meridian, called him by name, and asked him for help. Chaney's wrist, shoulder, and skull were crushed, as indicated by a New York doctor called in to examine the bodies. All three bodies were buried in darkness with a bulldozer. They were uncovered forty-four days later, with a bulldozer. The federal indictment charged that the three were let out of jail about 10:30 p.m., and they were murdered on June 21, 1964. The federal agents were convinced that the murder was done before midnight. The three bodies were tossed into the station wagon and driven along dirt roads to a farm about six miles southwest of Philadelphia. (The Perfect Burial Ground): (FBI MiBurn File: Mississippi Burn) "A cattle pond" was under construction on this farm. Erecting an earthen dam in a proper spot creates a pond. To begin building a dam you usually dig a ditch about 30 feet wide and 5 feet deep and 100 or more feet long. Into this ditch you pack red clay: it hardens and creates a base for the dam under which water will not seep. Onto the base for the dam under which water will not seep. Onto the base you then pile dirt, sloping the sides, to whatever height is needed. You plant grass along the sides. A finished dam may be 30 feet wide at the base, 10 feet wide at the top, 20 feet high, and 100 feet long, all erected on the red-clay base. Such a dam is a perfect place in which to hide bodies." Heavy rains fell during July, so by August 1 the dam was massive and grassed over—a permanent tomb for three bodies if nobody ever talked. After the burial, the station wagon was driven to a point fifteen miles northeast of Philadelphia, to the edge of the Bogue Chitto Swamp. It was doused with diesel fuel and burned. Traditionally, in race murders, bodies have been thrown into rivers and swamps in Mississippi. So the murderers, by burning the station wagon on the edge of Bogue Chitto Swamp, were leading the "federals" to begin by dragging the rivers and swamps. They got a real kick out of the fact that in the summertime the swamps were hot and the rivers were teeming with snakes, chiggers, and mosquitoes. "It tickles the hell out of me," one of the murderers said, "just to think of old J. Edgar's boys sweatin' out there in that swamp, with them chiggers, water moccasins and skeeters." They celebrated with drinking and handshakes, congratulating themselves on a job well done. It is reported that they met with an official of the state of Mississippi. "Well, boys," he said, "you've done a good job. You've struck a blow for the white man. Mississippi can be proud of you. You've let these agitatin' outsiders know where this state stands. Go home now and forget it with an additional warning: I'm looking each one of you in the eye and telling you this: the first man who talks is dead!" (William Bradford Huie, *Three Lives for Mississippi*).

The search for the three missing civil rights workers lasted forty-five days. During the first week of their disappearance, many leaders of the civil rights movement suspected that they had been killed. James Farmer (CORE leader) along with Dick Gregory, John Lewis, and George Raymond came to Meridian the same week that they went missing. They were refused entrance to the city limits of Neshoba County by the Highway Patrol roadblock. In July, Martin Luther King Jr. and other celebrities came to our freedom school in Meridian. There begun rumors that their disappearance had been staged to gain publicity and money for the Summer Project. Whites in connection with previous Southern race murders had voiced hoax theories. Some sentiments expressed were that if the killing had occurred, somehow it was the victims who had provoked the "killers." The victims had come in from the outside just to stir up troubles. Most of the people of Philadelphia did not want the bodies to be found, and they stood ready to protect and reward the killers. It was reported that even when the FBI's information led them to actual Klansman, the agent's job was still difficult. In the Neshoba case, the agent didn't have enough basic background information to con anyone. The case was eventually solved by use of informants. In a story published on September 30, 2007, it was reported that Hoover used the mob to solve the civil rights murders in 1964. A former FBI agent went on trial in mob-tied murders. In the steamy summer of 1964, with J. Edgar Hoover desperate to find the bodies of three slain civil rights workers in Mississippi, the FBI asked an unknown Brooklyn goon to beat the information out of a Ku Klux Klansman. The Justice Department couldn't have an FBI agent pistol whip a Klansman or scare him to death with a gun in his mouth, so they tapped Gregory Scarpa Sr., a secret mob informant and a Colombo soldier. In real-life "Mississippi Burning," Scarpa brought his gorgeous seventeen-year-old Brooklyn girlfriend down South with him. There remain several theories, however, it is said that the use of the mobster actually helped the FBI crack the case.

While They Were Missing

The political climate: They were abducted on Sunday, June 21, 1964. The following Friday, June 26, 1964, after their abduction, George Wallace declared his run for president of the United States. Our local newspaper the *Meridian Star* carried this story:

Gov. Johnson Sides with 'Bama Chief

Mississippi Gov. Paul Johnson backed up SOUTH WILL NAME NEXT PRESIDENT WALLACE TELLS 10,000 IN JACKSON—Jackson, Miss. Gov. George Wallace of Alabama here Thursday night telling a roaring crowd of 10,000 "the south will determine who is the next president of the United States." "Certainly I am a candidate for president," Wallace said. "I am running for president because I was born free. I want your children and mine and our posterity to be unencumbered by the manipulations of a soulless state. It's time the white people of our various states started bloc voting," said Johnson. "No president of this nation will be elected unless he pays attention to Mississippi and Alabama," he said. "The people are tired of being taken for granted and kicked around by the leaders of both national parties." Gov. Johnson sided with Wallace in saying "the South has no use for the liberals of either national parties, we want a choice—not of two liberals—but a clear cut choice between a liberal and a conservative..." Wallace called the 1954 school desegregation ruling by the US Supreme Court "ridiculous and asinine," and said "any person who made such a ruling should have a psychiatric examination..." It is noted that neither Wallace nor Johnson mentioned the disappearance of Schwerner, Chaney and Goodman. It is understandable that every conspirator and murderer left that Coliseum feeling that he had the approval of both Wallace and Johnson.

After the bodies were found, the memorial services coincided in time with the Neshoba County Fair. The fairground was within sight of the dam from which the bodies had been excavated.

Here is how the fair described it, in its official releases:(Chamber of Commerce)

"The historically famous Neshoba County Fair is the only campground fair in the United States. There have been others but they have long since passed from the scene… Located in a park-like setting eight miles from Philadelphia, Mississippi, the fairground is a small city of its own, patterned after the typical Southern town, with a square but without a courthouse. A giant-size open-air pavilion sites in the center of the "square. Cabins and house surround the square proving residents with campground facilities. There are more than 250 such houses-with more than 2000 patrons occupying them for the week of the fair…"Mississippi's Giant Houseparty!" The cabins are owned and built by the individuals families, many are maintained by those who have moved away years ago but make the annual pilgrimage back home for the fair"… The official release goes on to describe beauty pageant events, exhibits, livestock shows, grandstand shows, Western bands, picnics, Grand Ole Opry stars, etc., noting that nothing is left undone to provide a full week of entertainment—for young and old. No place is as exciting and different. In the political battleground of Mississippi, all prominent officeholders and political aspirants on the national and state levels considered the fair a must.

Evidently, it was a strong consideration for Ronald Reagan. In 1980, he announced his decision to run for president at this Neshoba County Fair as he sat in a rocking chair with a cowboy hat on. I recalled seeing that picture in the paper, and it left an indelible image that I find hard to dispel to this day.

Ronald Reagan won the Republican Party's nomination for president in 1980. The case was still a festering sore at that time. The local community was still protecting some of the conspirators, and white supremacy was still the order of the day. That was the atmosphere, and that was the place that Reagan chose as one of his first stops in his bid to run for president. He made his campaign debut at the Neshoba County Fair in front of a white and, at times, raucous crowd of perhaps ten thousand chanting,

"We want Reagan! We want Reagan!" Reagan was the first presidential candidate ever to appear at the fair, and he knew exactly what he was doing when he told that crowd, "I believe in states' rights." Everybody watching the 1980 campaign knew what Reagan was signaling at the fair. Whites and blacks, Democrats and Republicans—they all knew. The news media knew. The race haters and the people appalled by racial hatred knew. And Reagan knew. He was tapping out the code. It was understood that when politicians started chirping "states' rights" to white people in places like Neshoba County, they were saying that when it comes down to you and the blacks, we're with you. And Reagan meant it. He was opposed to the land-mark Civil Rights Act of 1964, which was the same year that Goodman, Schwerner, and Chaney were slaughtered. As president, he actually tried to weaken the Voting Rights Act of 1965. He opposed a national holiday for Reverend Dr. Martin Luther King Jr.[1]

The articles goes on to say: "For fundamental lovers of an old form of Americana—if you love 'folks' and want to go back to your 'raising,' this historically famous Neshoba County Campground Fair is the place to go."

Front Pages of Mississippi Papers Reflect the Climate/ Attitudes

"Civil Rights Steamroller Smashes on Measure Passes Senate 73–27"

"Strife and Chaos Forecast by Governor Johnson / Lt. Gov. Barnett: 'This action is repulsive to the American people. Turmoil, strife and bloodshed lie ahead.'"

"Gov. of Ala. George Wallace: Sad Day for Us. 'It is ironical that this event occurs as we approach celebration of Independence Day. On that day we won our freedom. On this day we have largely lost it.'"

It continues on Mississippi radio and television stations; there was nothing but angry voices and inflamed faces.

"Bloodshed! Strife! Turmoil! Chaos!"

When leaders predict strife and bloodshed, inevitably, among white-supremacist terrorists, they encourage strife and bloodshed.

---

[1] Bob Herbert, "Righting Reagan's Wrong?" *New York Times*, November 13, 2007.

The paper and local TV station WTOK ignored most civil rights news. The *Star* newspaper's acknowledgment of activities in the Meridian black community was limited to a regular column *In Colored Circles*, which listed births, weddings, illnesses, deaths, and names of out-of-town visitors.

The Search / FBI Involvement

The disappearance of James, Michael, and Andy immediately focused national attention on the Summer Project. The Justice Department was informed, but the FBI did not enter the case for more than a day. President Johnson authorized the use of two hundred sailors from the navy (including my fiancée) and at least 150 FBI agents in the search for the missing workers. Former CIA Director Allan Dulles and FBI Director J. Edgar Hoover visited the state to coordinate the effort. The incident did not result in basic change in federal policy regarding protection of civil rights workers. On August 4, 1964, the three bodies were found in an earth-fill dam near Philadelphia, Mississippi. They were missing for forty-four days before their bodies were discovered.

The Murder

What happened on the night of June 21, 1964? At least forty people, with the help of the law, committed a planned murder for the purpose of dramatizing Mississippi's defiance of the laws of the United States. "When the night is over, they'll know how Miss stands. They'll know we are not gonna take it! They're not gonna cram niggers into our schools or restaurants, and no more niggers are gonna vote in Miss. MLK may run the rest of the country, but he ain't gonna run Miss. And every Communist-atheist-nigger-loving-bearded-Jew-sonofabitch who comes down here looking for trouble is gonna find it!" Klan Leader: Bowers(footnote: Three Lives for Mississippi: William Bradford Huie)/FBI MiBurn Files).

From the FBI Reports:

According to the Klan's account, the "Jew boy" from New York was to be at the church in Longdale the same week that he (Mickey) was at the Oxford training school.

The Klan arrived at the Wednesday night prayer meeting and were disappointed that the "Jew boy" was not there. They made threats and disrupted the black worshipers' meeting. They arrived at the church to find only black parishioners. Using their disappointment as justification, they disrupted the prayer meeting and beat and harassed many of the church members. The Klan came prepared to eliminate the "Jew boy."

On Saturday, June 20, Mickey, J.E., and Andy returned to Meridian with the first wave of volunteers. The next day, June 21, the three drove to Neshoba County to meet with blacks about being beaten at the church and continuing the Summer Project. Sheriff Cecil Price, a member of the white knights of the KKK, stopped them for "speeding." Instead of giving them a ticket, he arrested them, placed them in the city jail in Philadelphia, and denied them phone calls while incarcerated and held incommunicado. Price contacted his KKK associates, and the Klan gathered. They arranged with Sheriff Lawrence Rainey to release the civil rights workers once an ambush had been set up on the road back to Meridian. Search procedures were initiated when they missed check-in time.

The three were released around 10:30 p.m. and told to "get of town." They were ambushed and turned over to the Klan murder mob. Price used the police siren. J.E. was savagely beaten, and all three were shot to death. On June 22, bodies were buried in an earthen dam on the property of a wealthy landowner, Olen Burrage. Their car was driven into Bogue Chitto Swamp and set on fire. By Tuesday, their disappearance had made the *New York Times*, and the burned car was discovered. Now Lyndon Johnson and the Feds woke up. The FBI and military search teams were ordered into action. LBJ met with the parents of Goodman and Schwerner, who came from New York to Washington DC. J.E.'s mother received no White House invitation.

Explanation of Why the Murders Took Place

William Bradford Huie made an analogy to the tyranny during Hitler's reign. He asks the question: was the entire state of Mississippi complicit?

"William Bradford Huie makes an analogy of the murder of these three martyrs to what took place in Germany during the reign of terror by Hitler: "When Terrorists murder with the complicity of the police, and when a society supports and cannot condemn them then the society or the state itself may be guilty. This was Nazi Germany's crime at Auschwitz; I was to discover that it was Mississippi's crime at Philadelphia."

Michael Schwerner, a young man who wanted to believe that there could never be another Auschwitz, drove his Volkswagen to Mississippi and found another Auschwitz before he reached his twenty-fifth birthday.

Author James W. Silver in his book *Mississippi: The Closed Society*, Professor Silver describes the white supremacist terrorists in these words:

In every Mississippi community there is an anxious, fearful, frustrated group of marginal white men. It makes no difference whether these people are suffering from their own personal inadequacies or whether they are overwhelmed by circumstances: they escape from their troubles periodically into the excitement of racial conflict. They are impelled to keep the Negro down in order to look up to themselves. Racial bigotry transcends reason in Mississippi because, for varying motives, so many leaders are willing to exploit the nameless dreads and alarms that have taken possession of most white people. The poor whites may not raise their low standard of living by blaming it on Negroes, but they do release an aggressive energy upon a socially accepted scapegoat. Themselves last in everything else, they can still rejoice in having the "nigger" beneath them. At least in the short run, nearly every white man does stand to derive economic, political, or social status from keeping Negroes in their place.

Kenneth Fairly of Jackson, Mississippi, and Harold Martin of Atlanta, Georgia, writing in the *Saturday Evening Post* of the Ku Klux Klan, said:

Deep angers and frustrations now motivate the Klansman. He is rebelling against his own ignorance, ignorance that restricts him to the hard and poorly paid jobs that are becoming scarcer every day. He is angered by the knowledge that the world is passing him by, that he is sinking lower and lower in the social order. The Negro is his scapegoat, for he knows that so long as the Negro can be kept "in his place," there will be somebody on the social and economic scale who is lower than he. In the Klavern (The Klan society), in his robes repeating the ancient ritual, he finds the status that is denied him on the outside.

It was well known that more than half of the "good, Christian white men" who planned Schwerner's murder and then exterminated the three had, within the preceding twelve months, been shown the old film *Birth of a Nation*. Klan organizers, like Robert Shelton carried prints of it and showed it in the lairs and Klaverns. The "gut sequence" of the film is a "pure white maiden" being run down and raped by a "big buck nigger."

Political/Social Climate in 1964

William Bradford Huie (*Three Lives for Mississippi*) asked the question of whether the three leading Southern political figures played a part in the murder of Goodman, Chaney, and Schwerner: The lieutenant governor of Mississippi Paul Johnson got the opportunity to stand in for then Mississippi Governor Barnett one evening due to his plane delay. Governor. Barnett had made a name for himself by defying federal marshals as they were ushering James Meredith onto the Ole Miss campus. He was the first black man to attempt to register in this all- white institution.

News photographers caught him defying federal marshals who were ushering James Meredith onto the Ole Miss Campus.

He stood on the podium and tried to outdo Barnett with the "nigger" jokes. He kept repeating the NAACP stands for "Niggers, Alligators, Apes, Coons, and Possums." This performance entertained, comforted, and encouraged the same people who later "activated Plan Four" against "The Jew-boy with the beard in Meridian." Huie further offers that George Wallace was himself a redneck. He was born between plow handles and was well acquainted with the south end of a northbound mule. He knew the feel of patches on his britches and warm cow dung between his toes. He was twisted by hate and sick with ambition. And he, too, knew the taste of defeat. The year 1962 was his last chance to be governor, so he had one campaign cry: "Nigger, nigger, nigger, and god dam Earl Warren!" Wallace comforted every Klansman in Alabama and Mississippi, for his picture was displayed in lairs all over as "the Great Leader of the White Man's Cause." Wallace's administration will be remembered for the release of the castrators of Edward Aaron, for his trying to bar two qualified citizens of Alabama from the state university because they were born black, and for his part in increasing the Negro vote through the horrifying brutality displayed at Selma. Perhaps governors who comfort terrorists should not be blamed for their crimes. But should they be held blameless?[2]

On January 7, 2005, four decades after the crime, Edgar Ray Killen, eighty, was charged with three counts of murder. He was accused of orchestrating the killings and assembling the mob that killed the three men. On June 21, the forty-first anniversary of the murder, Killen was convicted of three counts of manslaughter, a lesser charge. He received the maximum sentence, sixty years in prison. The grand jury declined to call for the arrest of the seven other living members of the original group of eighteen suspects arrested in 1967, one being the grandfather of a former Miss America from Meridian, Mississippi (Susan Akin, 1986).

A major reason the case was reopened was a 1999 interview with Sam Bowers, a former Ku Klux Klan grand wizard convicted in 1967 of giving the order to have Michael Schwerner killed. (I walked the streets of Meridian with Mickey daily, oblivious to the danger that he was in.)

In Meridian, Bowers remarked in the interview that took place more than thirty years after the crime. "I was quite delighted to be convicted and have the main instigator of the entire affair walk out of the courtroom a free man. Everybody, including the trial judge and the prosecutors and everyone else, knows that that happened." Bowers, a grand wizard of the KKK, claims that Killen was a central figure in the murders and organized the KKK mob that carried them out. (Bowers is currently serving a life sentence for ordering a 1966 firebombing in Hattiesburg, Mississippi, that killed Vernon Dahmer, a Mississippi civil rights leader, another crime that took decades to successfully prosecute) The murders of James Chaney, Andrew Goodman, and Michael Schwerner. Info Please by: Borgna Brunner

The Arrest

Several months later, twenty-one white men, including the sheriff of Neshoba County and one of his deputies were arrested. They were charged with conspiracy to deprive the dead men of their civil rights. The federal government then stepped in, and the FBI arrested eighteen men in

---

[2] William Bradford Huie, *Three Lives for Mississippi.*

connection with the killings. In 1967, seven white men were convicted and sentenced to three to ten years, but one served more than six. No one was charged for murder.

In October 1964, the FBI arrested eighteen men, but state prosecutors refused to try the case, claiming lack of evidence. This was the contemptible version of justice at the time: "They killed one nigger, one Jew and a white man. I gave them all what I thought they deserved." They were all-white juries, and another three ended in mistrials. Another eight defendants were acquitted. One of those mistrials freed Edgar Ray "Preacher" Killen, -believed to be the ringleader, after the jury in his case was deadlocked by one member who said she couldn't bear to convict a preacher.

Source: FBI File: MiBurn (Mississippi Burn)

Justice Updates: (June 13, 2005)

Jury selection opened in Philadelphia, Mississippi, in the murder trial of Edgar Ray Killen. Killen watched the proceedings from a wheelchair he has used since he broke his legs in a tree-cutting accident in March. Security was tight with streets around the courthouse barricaded. Ben Chaney, the brother of murder victim James Chaney, told reporters he found the prosecution encouraging. Other civil rights observers complained, however, that other surviving conspirators, such as Olen Burrage, should be facing charges as well.

(June 23, 2005)

Judge Marcus Gordon sentenced Edgar Ray Killen to serve three twenty-year terms, one for each conviction of manslaughter in connection with the deaths of Chaney, Goodman, and Schwerner in 1964. Judge Gordon said in pronouncing sentence, "I have taken into consideration that there are three lives in this case and that the three lives should be absolutely respected." Sentencing followed Killen's conviction earlier in the week. The manslaughter convictions came after nearly three days of jury deliberations. The jury found that there was reasonable doubt as to whether Killen intended that the Klansmen kill the civil rights workers and thus did not return a murder conviction.

(November 2007)

Linda Schiro, the ex-girlfriend of former mobster Gregory Scarpa, nicknamed "The Grim Reaper," testifying for the prosecution in a murder case, stated that Scarpa put a gun in the mouth of a Ku Klux Klansman in an effort to gain information about the location of the bodies of Chaney, Schwerner, and Goodman. The ploy worked, and the bodies were soon dug up in an earthen dam. Scarpa died in prison in the 1990s.

Schiro's story confirmed reports coming from confidential FBI sources in 1994 that a frustrated J. Edgar Hoover had turned to the Colombo crime family for help in cracking the "Mississippi Burning" case.

(August, 2008)- Jimmy Arledge died in 8/2008.

(August 2009)

On August 13, 2009, Billy Wayne Posey died at age seventy-three. Alejandro Miyar, a spokesperson for the Department of Justice, said that Posey's death does not "alter our cold-case investigation." Four suspects in the 1964 murders remain alive.

2009-Billy Wayne Posey died Owner of Phillip 66 Garage lived at 4529 Kings Rd-Meridian, Ms.

(March 2013)- On March 15, Owen Burrage died at the age of eighty-two. Burrage owned the farm on which Goodman, Chaney, and Schwerner were buried under an earthen dam. He was acquitted in the 1967 trial. Days before the killings, Burrage bragged that his 250-foot long dam would make a good burial place for civil rights workers. According to an FBI informant, Burrage told a roomful of KKKers discussing the arrival of the civil rights workers in 1964, "Hell, I've got a dam that will hold a hundred of them." Horace Barnette told the FBI that around midnight after the killings, Burrage was waiting at his farm to direct Klansmen to the dam site. Burrage then went to his trucking company garage to get the gasoline that was used to burn the civil rights workers' station wagon. With the death of Burrage, only one of the eighteen people originally indicted remains alive. The survivor is Pete Harris, whom witnesses say called the Klansmen to gather on the night of the murders.

Wayne Roberts:

Wayne Roberts was the triggerman. He killed Schwerner, Goodman, and Chaney on Rock Cut Road on the night of June 21, 1964. He was identified at trial as the killer by fellow Klansman James Jordan. Roberts was convicted and sentenced to ten years in prison by Judge Cox. Roberts served his sentence at the federal penitentiary in Leavenworth, Kansas. He later found work in a car dealership in Meridian.

Roberts was a rough and rowdy twenty-six-year-old ex-marine in 1964. He was dishonorably discharged from the marines for fighting, drunkenness, and being absent without leave. He was, by many accounts, "as mean as a junkyard dog." He worked in Meridian as a window salesman.

Roberts began loudly calling for Schwerner's execution soon after joining the Lauderdale County Klan. Roberts was among the Klan members who participated in the beating of blacks at the Mount Zion Church on June 16. He seemed especially proud of his brutal deed, raising his bloody fist in the air as proof of his work.

Even after his arrest as one of nineteen conspirators in December 1964, Roberts was a man to avoid. After a hearing in 1965, Roberts raced across a courthouse yard to kick a CBS cameraman in the groin and then slug him in the head.

November/2013 -Edgar Ray Killen, an outspoken white supremacist, and considered the orchestrator of the conspiracy was found guilty of three counts of manslaughter on June 21, 2005. He was sentenced to sixty years in prison-twenty years for each count, served consecutively.

In November 2013, he made another attempt to appeal this ruling, but was rejected by the U.S. Supreme Court, and is serving 60 years in a Mississippi prison.

2014- There are three conspirators still living at end of this writing:

#1-Pete Harris lives in Meridian, Ms.

#2-Jimmy Townsend resides in Philadelphia, Ms.

#3-Edgar Ray Killin is serving a 60-year prison term.

Clarion Ledger Investigative Reporter of Jackson, Ms, still researching Killers today.

Email Jmitchell@jackson.gannett.com

CHAPTER EIGHT

Coping:

"Just My Imagination Running away with me" (The Temptations)

"A silent partner is someone always there for you; you may take their presence for granted. It is a presence that you don't often miss until it is gone forever. A silent partner will faithfully support, encourage, and watch your back whether you are looking or not". (Bernice Sims)

I became their silent partner as a way of coping while they were being held in the Neshoba County Jail. My imagination was running away with me. I have dreamed, re-dreamed, fantasized and became haunted by the memory of their impending deaths. I have seen them in their final hours in jail separated from each other. I didn't need to see the movie Mississippi Burning. I had my own internal film. I am reminded of the crucifixion of Christ. The FBI reports that J.E. was beaten senseless before being nailed to a cross for all to see. The act of crucifixion was in itself a form of humiliation. The Klan's leader marked them for elimination months before their abduction. You have to wonder why they felt the necessity to humiliate them by segregated jail cells. It was a system that defiles love and God with no regard for life, liberty, or human rights. I have seen them and imagined what they were discussing as the time passed away. I have seen Mickey's optimism fading with the lingering hours coupled with being denied telephone privileges. I've seen his optimism being revisited upon them after receiving food from the gatekeeper's wife. This tiny gesture of human kindness provided hope and faith. I have seen them waiting on someone to post bail and come to their aid as had happened in the past. I have been there in the cell with them, seeing Andy's face so confused and frightened by the whole incident and J.E. being in a segregated cell, frightened and alone because he fully understood his fate. His past experience with the Klan as a black Mississippian had taught him how they operate. He had lost a love—one due to Klan activities in the South. I see his frustration at being alone and separated in this his last hours from those with whom he had bonded, those to whom he would be forever bonded. They were separated by the same vehicle (racism) that had brought them together. The evil of racism was exemplified in the worst mockery of it's kind-being denied one's last hours of life by a system that excludes human contact between two races—. A system in which white supremacy can feel justified and arrogant enough to disregard anything that they do not sanction according to their ways of doing things. They operate on their unnatural laws and their relentless pursuit to maintain the rules of white supremacy. It is the ultimate insult, being denied an opportunity to touch your last breath of humanity. I have been able to see just how it happened. I left with them that day. I have relived it step by step and followed them to their deaths. I have seen them in their last hours in that jail cell. I've seen, and imagined what they were discussing. I've seen Mickey's hope and optimism rise from time to time, because he always told me that he believed in the goodness of men. When tested he said, "Man would rise to the occasion of goodness". You may say that this was his religious belief, as we discussed it often. He was probably comforted in knowing that someone was coming to bail them out? He didn't know that their whereabouts were unknown. I have been there in the cell with them, seeing Andy's face so confused by the whole incident on his first full day in the state of Mississippi. He had probably only seen a handful of people outside of my family. It was Father's Day, and he had made plans to call his father in New York. I know because he told me about those plans when I last saw him. It must have been so surreal to him. What must J.E. be feeling now in this isolation? So alone and segregated from Mickey and Andy. Alone and frightened because he was probably now fully comprehending their fate. His past experience with the Klan has provided him knowledge of their modus operandi. He was probably aware that those lingering hours in the jail were allowing the Klan time to organize and collect themselves. Did he try to get word to them on the other side of the jailhouse, or did he just keep this to himself? I wonder. The Klan always committed their most heinous and cowardly acts of violence at night. They had gotten arrested around

4:00 p.m, according to published reports. I recall what my Dad said before leaving for work on the evening shift. He talked about feeling elated over the spiritual encounter that he had witnessed with the trio. He remembered it so well. He shared with me a few months before he died that he found Mickey's sermon to be very uplifting. Dad said, "I didn't feel like I missed church at all on Father's Day." He told me how much he hated to leave us because everyone was having such a good time listening to Mickey. He thought that Mickey had perfect pitch and good cadence and he was surprised that J.E. had such a good singing voice. He thought that Mickey could rival the Baptist minister that we heard preaching over the radio. Was Mickey teasing my mother? Or was he really being affected by the sermon? We will never know. I can see J.E.'s frustration at being alone and isolated in these final hours without his friend that he had grown to love, and a new colleague that he felt so well connected. This vehicle of ignorance and hatred would separate them forever as they lay waiting in their jail cells —One for blacks and one for whites. This is another evil of racism, and the course it took in their lives.

It is a mockery of a sort, being denied in your final hours of life by a system that chooses to deny a human touch. A system that allows one to feel justified and arrogant enough to disregard anything not sanctioned according to their ways of doing things. Their unnatural laws, in relentless pursuit to maintain white supremacy. The Sheriff's wife brought them their last meal. Did they feel much like eating? I have imagined what it would have been like if I or my brothers had gone. I have imagined that if I had gone, the outcome would have been different. I have imagined that I could have talked Mickey into letting me go with them had I reached the car in time. Gee, I had tagged along with him so many times in the past. I could always get him to change his mind about taking me with him. I have imagined that I could have averted the tragedy. Maybe seeing a young black girl would have caused the Klan to abort their plans. This was only a fantasy that comes along with the collective guilt that I felt. Knowing full well that, if I had gone, it would have been four or, even five people lynched that day if my brother had chosen to accompany them. The survivor guilt is still quite prevalent in my family. Marshall feels responsible for encouraging J.E. to take on the field representative role that he held for a short time. He left Mississippi, and went north after so much harassment from the local police. He felt that he had influenced J.E. to replace him as field representative. Marshall is so overcome with guilt that he cannot see or talk about James, Andy, or Mickey to this day. He refuses to attend anniversaries or reunions for the civil rights workers. No one can measure the toll of any one's death. It is even harder to comprehend deaths that are untimely and unrighteous. Especially those that are based upon someone who has decided that they have the right to play God. When we realized that the trio was missing, many thought that they would not be found alive. Around our home, we tried to keep up a brave face because my mother was holding onto to hope. Deep inside, we knew that the worst had probably happened as we reflected upon how they had attacked the church people. The full impact did not faze me, even though I recalled that our home had been swamped with news correspondents. Several people came to our home and identified themselves as writers, and report-ers asking numerous questions about the trio's state of mind before they left our home. We were very young, and still very much in shock and disbelief. I know that my mother held onto hope until their bodies were discovered. We came to understand that these reporters had been told that my family was among some of the last people to see them alive before they left for Neshoba County. I remember vaguely that a newsperson identified himself as a writer of the Saturday Evening Post. I distinctly remember him telling me where his particular article about the disappearance would be published. I remem-ber hearing names like Newsweek, Saturday Evening Post, the Atlantic and several magazines that sounded familiar. I'm sure that many misrepresented themselves to this southern family with limitations in matters of media and law enforcement. While they were missing, many well known leaders and office holders from coordinated civil rights organizations begun to come into Mississippi to participate in the search: Dr. Martin Luther King, John Lewis, Dick Gregory, Jim Forman, and Bob Moses, Rev. Jesse Jackson, and other known activists and celebrities. All of the local and national attention made it harder to hold onto hope. In spite of all of the mixed emotions that we were feeling, we tried to continue to keep a brave face. There was work to be done, and we could honor them by fulfilling the mandate that we had started on the MFDP. There were so many depressed expressions at the Community center as we tried to stick to the scheduled plans for the summer. We held the statewide convention in Meridian for all of the freedom schools. I worked on two committees for the event: registration and hospitality. It was at one of our community meetings that we received the news that we most dreaded. Civil Rights Activist and Folk Singer, Pete Seeger was performing for us on August 4, 1964. He interrupted his performance, and gave us the news that the bodies of our fallen comrades had been located in Neshoba County. There were gasps, expressions of shock, and groins of pain among the students and guest. He paused for a few minutes, returned to the microphone, and slowly begun to lead us in singing our anthem: We Shall Overcome Someday, Deep in my heart, I do Believe, We shall overcome someday through our windows of tears. I then recalled something that I saw on the three martyrs faces on the day in which they left. There was such peace, contentment and resolution. I drew strength from this and wanted to continue the work ahead of us. The work for the (MFDP) Mississippi Freedom Democratic Party for the convention to be held during the last week of August. There was such chaos as we juggled emotions within the throes of our disbelief, shock, and pain. Years later, I discovered that my fiancée, who was part of the Naval search team had been swore to secrecy for statements that he made to his commanding officer. Statements about my work within the organization that I was not privy, due to his military status. Some of the information given was not all accurate. I never talked about any of my activities with him because I had been cautioned that it represented a conflict being political and serving in the military. He had to report to his commanding officer information that he was indirectly connected to the missing trio via his fiancée, but unsure of my exact role in the movement. When I realized that they were gone forever, I think that I allowed a part of me to die along with them. So much of my enthusiasm got buried in the earthen grave along with them. I remember not caring about what happened to me. Many of my dreams and aspirations left. All of the fire had been extinguished. It didn't matter that my young husband betrayed me with his promise to send me to college. When he said, "No. What do you think that I am, a fool? Do you think that I would fatten a frog for a snake? No, I will not help you to go to college." I was disappointed and relieved at the same time. It really didn't matter anymore—not too much did. I heard it as an echo of relief. Now, I had words, validation, and a comforter to my soul, a spirit to rest. I had words to put to my relief. Someone said, "No," an authority figure, someone I was supposed to listen to, my husband. In those days, we took our vows about obeying very seriously. It helped to substantiate my role—one that had a fleeting presence. Now I had something to replace the activism and creativity in my soul. I had a role. I was now married with a husband. Now, I was the wife of a military man. I had a direction to move toward.

CHAPTER NINE
Coming to Terms:

I am sure that I felt guilty for many years because I did not attend the funeral for JE, Mickey or Andy. I even broke contact with everyone involved. It was as though everything that had happened was a dream, and the reality of their deaths was the nightmare, a nightmare that I still found myself awakening from at times. Sometimes, I'd awaken in a cold sweat and crying. At times, I would begin to fantasize a palatable, idealized relationship with the whole thing that would allow me to become their savior.

Denial and Disbelief:

It took me ten years to be able to read any accounts of their murder. I don't know how long I could have continued operating in the denial. However, a series of events forced me to confront my denial and pain: two books, a television special, a movie, and a commemorative reunion. I read Ann Moody's "Coming of Age in Mississippi", and recognized names of early civil rights workers whom I had become acquainted. Mathieu's Suarez (Flukie). He later became one of our Youth leaders. In reading, William B. Huie's: "Three Lives for Mississippi", my brothers were mentioned as the student barbers who gave them haircuts on the day of their disappearance. In some writings, my brothers and I were referred to as the three Sims associated with pre-Freedom summer activism. One could get the impression that we were thought of as all being males. It was my home and my brothers that I was reading about. The full impact didn't hit me until many years later. My family and I had an association with one of the most heinous crimes in the history of civil rights. Coming to terms with writing about this part of that history was an arduous process that took years. Every time I'd think about that day, it was painfully overwhelming. It was like reliving the pain and loss all over again each time I sat down to write. How often can a person keep putting herself through that kind of pain? I found that I was only able to discuss the intimate details of the last time that we saw them alive was with close friends.

One day a good friend said to me, you have just told me the whole story, I think that you should write it down just for yourself. I followed her suggestion, and just put everything in writing. I felt that a tremendous burden had been lifted when I finished. However, that was only the beginning of a series of emotional encounters associated with grief and mourning that was to follow. I just started out by avoiding anything and anyone who reminded me of that day, and if I could, I'd run away. There was the visual stimulus, which caused a strong emotional reaction in 1977. I saw Rita, Mickey's widow on a PBS Special entitled: Thirteen years after the civil rights murders in Miss. I left the room where the TV was playing, and later returned. I listened to some of the documentary, while seeing her face. It was good to see her again. My leaving the room did not erase the visual. I did reach out to Rita, and we had a warm conversation. I could not get beyond thinking, that my reaching out would only evoke painful memories. We exchanged current contact information, however, I didn't see her again until 2005. I accepted an invitation to attended the 41-year commemorative Reunion, in Neshoba County in 2005. At this event in Philadelphia, Ms, I saw and embraced Mickey's widow and James Chaney's brother, Ben for the first time in over 41 years. I spoke publicly at this event. It was the same year that Edgar Ray Killin was brought to trial as the orchestrating conspirator for the trio's murder. I also visited Jackson, Miss to see the memorial site for the slain Civil Rights Leader, Medgar Evers. I could easily recognize the commemorative neighborhood site. It was as I had remembered it on my last visit in 1963. I was overcome with an eerie feeling that time had just stood still.

In 1988, another reminder was the movie, "Mississippi Burning". My son came running into to house to inform me he saw a movie trailer about my lost friends. I couldn't hear him because almost simultaneously, I saw the movie trailer come up on my TV set. I found myself frantically searching for my keys and running for the door. I needed to get outside of my home because there was no air. I couldn't breathe. I could not tolerate looking at the scene being played out on the screen: The heavy chains pulling that familiar station wagon from the swamps of Philadelphia, Miss. I ran for the door, into my street, feeling nausea and gasping for air. I was pleased that my neighborhood was practically deserted after 9 PM. That way, no one would have to see me releasing stomach content of what appeared to be everything from within me. To this day, I am still unable to watch the Mississippi Burning.

In 1989, I received a phone call at my place of employment from Andrew Goodman's mother. She identified herself and shared with me that she had wanted to ask me about something that had haunted her for years. She wanted to know if her son had gotten any sleep before his abduction and murder. I had to provide an answer to one of the hardest question that I've ever been asked. She had pondered over this because she had traced the time line to our home after they left the Ohio training site.

She told me that she had discovered that we were some of the last people who had seen them alive. She also knew about their arrival time in Meridian on June 20, 1964. I could only answer based upon what they told us. They had driven all night in order to avoid problems with those thought to be enemies against the movement. They told us about driving all night from Ohio to reach the Mississippi line before daylight.

I accepted an invitation to attend a twenty-fifth reunion of Freedom Summer Workers in Queens, New York in 1989. I was on the dais with Rosa Parks and James Chaney's sister, Barbara Chaney. Barbara and I reminisced about some of the good times we shared growing up as next-door neighbors. We exchanged numbers, as we were both living in New York. However, we never reached out to each other. It was a sobering reunion as I walked among many familiar faces. I reconnected with some workers who had been assigned to the Meridian Freedom School. Mark Levy, our Director, who also lives in New York, was among them. He gave me his contact information, and spoke about others, and their whereabouts. He gave me photos from the freedom school along with school reports, and copies of the class schedule; curricula. We managed to touch base a few times after that event. It remains difficult to reach out to those closely involved in our youth group. Some of us know how to locate each other; we try from time to time, but still find it difficult to reach out and touch. I guess because we think that it will still hurts too much.

These chains of events made it even more difficult for my memories to remain buried. I had to dig myself out of the emotional grave that I was hiding in, and revisit the trauma of my loss. Keeping it to myself was somehow protecting something that I didn't have to share, something that I could keep for myself, and for us alone. Something that could be safe, and ours. "Mickey, JE, an Andy, I could give you the safety that no one was able to give you on June 21, 1964." "I could keep you Safe from your executors". I came to realize that I had to write the book to complete my own grief process.

I did not research any articles until many years later. I found myself spending hours at the Forty-Second Street and Fifth Avenue Library in New York City, going through what would be by now, considered their archives. I had been haunted about what I would uncover in my research. I read so many articles and stories, and after a while, I was unable to comprehend all that I was reading.

I was unable to find anything about what their mood was like that day before they died. I never read anything in the reports that Mickey and Andy had fresh haircuts and J.E.'s endless teasing of me, which had been his pattern. I didn't read anything about how proudly J.E. talked about looking forward to seeing his baby daughter. He talked a lot about being more than ever devoted to the "cause" because he was now doing this for her, his baby girl. How much he wanted a better life for her! I keep hearing him say: "Man, I got a baby girl, and I am doing this for her" over and over again that morning at my home. We were under the impression that he had seen her before coming to our home. There was nothing in those articles or reports that talked about what a good time Andy was having on the porch playing cards and constructing string games with my younger brother. There was nothing in the reports about how Mickey and my mother were arguing about religion, and how he was preaching and mimicking the Baptist preacher, singing praises to God and shouting hallelujah and amen louder than the "hellfire and damnation" radio preacher.

There was nothing that I could find in the reading that expressed the happiness and peace in Mother's face when she had converted Mickey to Christianity.

If he was playing with my mother, then he deserved an Academy Award, because to this day, we are all confused. We don't know if he was sincere or joking with Mother. All that I can say is that they had argued so many times before and it ended with neither giving up an inch on their point of view. I read nothing about how much they enjoyed eating Mama's fried chicken and cupcakes. I read in the FBI reports how they didn't have enough money to pay a twenty-dollar speeding fine, which was used as the justification to arrest them. All I could remember was that Mickey had sent me to the store to cash a twenty-dollar bill, I returned with $19.50. I went to the store to get change so that he could pay the fifty-cent cost for his haircut. I personally went to the corner, Cross Store, at Mickey's request to get the change for him. I didn't buy anything, as he suggested. I spent only enough in order to get the shopkeeper to make change from the $20 bill. My goal was just to get Mickey's twenty-dollar bill changed so I could return most of it to him. I knew he was going on this mission to Neshoba County, and I figured he might need it, although he had told me to purchase whatever I wanted.

You can image the pain, anger, and confusion I felt, because I knew that between the three of them, they had enough money to pay for the trumped-up traffic violation that they had been charged with. There was nothing that I could read about how they tried to persuade my brothers Marshall and David to go with them to Neshoba County. Both had tried to get them to come back later for them. I didn't read anything about how I pleaded to go with them, and the angry I felt upon losing the male chauvinism argument. There was little satisfaction for me satiating myself on stories about their deaths. I read the FBI reports that left out things that I remembered. I realized after a while that I couldn't find what I was looking for in my research when I decided to write about that day. What I was looking for could only be found within me.

CHAPTER TEN

Current Political Climate:

Chaney, Goodman, and Schwerner died because they were trying to help blacks in the South to have a voice in the voting booths. We find that even today, those rights are being threatened nearly fifty years after they made the ultimate sacrifice.

2012: There is a case under consideration by the Supreme Court in which the State of Alabama is challenging the 1965 Voting Rights Act. This law was put into place to protect newly registered black voters in Southern states, who have been historically denied the right to vote. It offers protection from intimidation at the polls. The 2012 election appeared at times to be destined to be marred by blatant attempts to suppress the minority vote through voter ID laws and other devices, such as long lines at the polls deliberately orchestrated by state legislatures to suppress the vote. An ugly reminder is the face of a ninety-three-year-old black woman named Desiline Victor having to wait in line for over three hours because voting hours were cut in her state.

The landmark Voting Rights Act of 1965 is again under a legal microscope. The Supreme Court, with its right-leaning justices, is considering revisiting the constitutionality of the law. The court agreed to hear a challenge by an Alabama county that wants to void the law's requirement that certain voting districts get clearance from the Justice Department before changing election rules or procedures. There was good reason for that requirement. Congress approved the Voting Rights Act to stop officials in all or part of sixteen states with a history of discrimination from disenfranchising minority voters through a variety of tactics. A commonly used tactic is putting polling places in locations inconvenient to minority groups or drawing voting districts to dilute their strength. Critics say the law is a relic of the Jim Crow era, which steps on the sovereign rights of the states. They feel that the progress that the South has made in race relations since 1965 invalidates the need for the law. The law's opponents make a point in saying the South of Bull Connor and church bombings is long gone, but that doesn't mean the voters are always treated equally. Just look at the recent efforts by the opposition party in a number of states, including Pennsylvania, that tried to use ID laws to discourage minorities from showing up on Election Day. The reality reveals that federal oversight is still the best tool in many situations to thwart attempts to suppress voting. The Justice Department has had the occasion to use the Voting Rights Act to successfully block restrictive voter ID laws in South Carolina and Texas, which might have kept many minority voters from exercising their rights in the 2012 election. The declared intent of voter ID laws is to prevent fraud at polling places. But their proponents have yet to provide a shred of evidence that voter impersonation is a problem anywhere. Congress has repeatedly renewed the Voting Rights Act, most recently in 2006, when it extended its clearance requirement for twenty-five years. Three years ago, the court decided by an eight-to-one margin in another case to leave the clearance section intact, but the justices also indicated its days may be numbered. Congress left the law's opponents an opening for a new challenge. The court has been signaling its lack of patience with civil rights–era laws and policies that it feels should be near the end of their shelf life. The thinking is that those twenty-five years should complete the life span. But as the 2012 election showed, reaching that point is still a goal, not an accomplishment. The state argued that we are living in a different time and that law is unnecessary. We all fought to secure a rightful place at the polling booth in a war that left many victims; many have been unable to come to grips with their lives as a result of visible and invisible scars from violence and intimidation experienced at the hands of the white supremacists.

The fights, the struggles, and the losses endured during the sixties were too arduous and painful to have to repeat. Does each generation have to fight the civil war? The 1965 Voting Rights Act gave one the right to vote without having to be harassed at polling places.

Unfortunately, it had a shelf life and was not intended to last forever. In addition to that oversight, now, in over thirty-four states, voter suppression laws have raised their ugly head. It is estimated that voter suppression could have affected nearly five million voters in the 2012 election. There is nothing more fundamental to our democracy than the right to vote. New laws that have passed around the country that restrict the pool of eligible voters and make it harder for Americans to cast a ballot represent a step backward in a decades-long struggle to end discrimination in this country. We don't want America to turn back the clock on the fundamental right to vote.

Harry Belafonte, in a documentary on HBO in 2009/2010, recently said, "I never thought that I was trying to fix things that I thought I fixed over fifty years ago. I am still working in LA with Cripps and Bloods, trying to help alleviate the violence. This fact still confounds me." Voter suppression laws, the minimizations of women's rights, and the resurgence of anti-black, Hispanic, gay, and women efforts confound me as well."

Rhode Island, Wisconsin, Tennessee. Ohio, South Carolina, Texas, and Florida are among the states that have instituted new regulations regarding voting—e.g., requiring voter ID cards and restrictions on early and absentee voting. The opposition party has engaged in a substantial effort to change the voting laws in individual states to give an advantage to their side in the upcoming presidential and other elections. Legislative action sponsored by the current dominant Republican-led state legislatures is making it harder for voters to cast ballots.

Yes, this is happening in the year 2012. In Florida, the sitting Governor has passed a House Bill 1355 which requires voter registration group to pre-register with state before engaging in any voter's registration activity, all registration material must be delivered within 48 hours of voter's signatures. Monthly reports must be filled with state restrictions on early/absentee ballot, executive action making it harder to restore voting rights taken restriction on voter's registration passed. All done in an effort to give their party an unfair advantage. Sunday voting restrictions before election and voter's identification will effect minorities, the elderly and student.

The voter suppression initiatives of today will create the same results as the Jim Crow laws of the 1960s did. They will ensure the absence of your voice and deny you the right to participate in the democratic process. Voter's rights, human rights, women's rights, gay rights, etc.—the beat goes on…We must continue the fight for voter's rights, equal pay for women, gay/lesbian rights, and full citizenships for undocumented immigrants, etc. The beat goes on….

The opposition party has engaged in a substantial effort to change the voting laws in individuals' states to give an advantage to their side in the 2012 presidential and other elections. Legislative action sponsored by the current dominant political party led state legislature is making it harder for voters to cast ballot.

April, 2014: the sitting Gov of Wisconsin signed a bill which allow poll watchers to stand as close as three feet away from a potential voter. A well funded organization called "True to Vote: has been notorious is using intimidation surveillance tactics challenging voters as they exercise their right to vote.

President Obama's election and reelection in 2012, seem to have ignited the movement of the sixties all over again: civil rights, voting inequities, and women and immigration rights.

Battles that we thought that we had fought and won we find ourselves in the middle of again some of the same battles. I have asked myself, "Have I just awakened from a deep sleep like Rip van Winkle? Have I been asleep for almost fifty years instead of twenty like Mr. van Winkle?"

Upon the fifty-year anniversary of my colleague's deaths, perhaps we can answer the question of whether my friends died in vain. Were they victims, or was there a victory? We can celebrate their lives and honor their deaths with a newfound activism giving testimony to their heroism. We are nearing the fiftieth anniversary of their tragic deaths. They were committed idealists, willing to put their lives on the line to fight for what they believed in, and to right the wrongs of past injustices. We still need that kind of youthful passion and energy to keep the world alert because what was fought for and won can easily be taken or stolen. We must remain vigilant, and we cannot rely upon the past accomplishments. The trumpet is sounding loudly for a new generation to move to the front again.

Melissa Harris-Perry, a professor of political science at Tulane University and MSNBC TV host, shared a story in an early TV promo. She stated that she found it puzzling that her dad would always sign her birthday and special cards with: "The struggle continues, Love, Daddy," as opposed to just "Love, Daddy." Her father was born in the Jim Crow South. She said that she had since learned the meaning of this unusual closing. He was conveying to her that many of the racial problems have persisted for years and many people who came before you have been working on them; in your lifetime, you will have to take up the banner and do your part to continue the fight for equal rights and justice. Many of society's ills can't be resolved in one's lifetime, and many continue to persist today. She was able to understand that all generations will have to struggle for equal rights, and each generation must do its fair share. There have been many people before you, who have fought and paid the ultimate price for the freedom that allows us to walk freely into a polling place and vote and for civil rights. You don't have to solve all the problems in your lifetime. Your job is to take up the banner and pass it on to others in the next generation. Dr. Harris-Perry's father was born in the Jim Crow South and fought for many of the same rights that we thought that we had won. Now, we find ourselves almost fifty years later fighting for those same rights again.

I must admit that hearing this from Professor Harris-Perry gave me some comfort as I find myself being anguished, distressed, and frustrated over the present state of affairs, especially in the neo–voter suppression techniques used to obtain an unfair advantage and deny others the opportunity to exercise their rights to vote. You must take up the banner as you are presented with some of the same challenges. The world that we live in does not permit apathy. Apathy destroys us all. The trumpet is sounding loudly for a new generation to move to the front of the line and fight again.

4/10/14 *"History travels not only forward, but backward, History is not guaranteed to travel forward."(President Barack Obama speaking at the 50th Commemorative celebration for LBJ (President Lyndon B. Johnson) honoring him for his signature Domestic legislation: The passing of 1964 Civil Rights Bill signed on July 2, 1964.*

"I Hear a Symphony" (The Supremes)

I am pleased to hear about the Coalition of Activists: the Dream Keepers and the Moral Mondays. They continue to hold their heads high in the fight for voter and human rights.

EPILOGUE:

Grief/The Real Freedom Summer:

"When a murder is committed, you can never predict the farthest reaches of its tentacles into the universe."(Bernice Sims).

James, Michael, and Andrew left my home alive and in good spirits on that dreadful Father's Day in June, of 1964.

Discovering that I had been among some of the last people to see them alive carries a heavy burden. You are haunted with survival guilt because you don't feel worthy. You feel ashamed, because you think that this privilege should have been reserved for the immediate families. You feel like a thief, like you stole something that didn't belong to you. You then keep those memories inside, so you don't have to deal with the negative emotions associated with them. I came to realize that by not releasing those emotions were also connected with my attempt to keep my friends safe from harm. I kept the ones that I knew about safely in my memory bank never to be tampered with until I was forced. I felt blocked and often lost my creativity because I was always dealing with so much pain, hurt lost and guilt. I tried to bury all of the memories along side them in their earthen grave. The Trio and I shared good times on that fateful day of June 21, 1964. I had failed to talk about those times. The pain and sense of loss was so overwhelming that I couldn't think of the good times. The Good times needed to be shared with others who remember only the pain.

Closing thoughts: The Real Freedom Summer:

I often wondered why my mother allowed us to get involved so early in a movement that was so unpredictable and dangerous. I asked her why she allowed us to participate and place our family at risk. Our home was well known to be one of the "host homes" during the Freedom Summer Movement. We welcomed all of the new recruits into our home. We interacted with a different type of white person than the predictable ones known to us in the south. In the south, the expectations were that we were supposed to be subservient-conditioned. Mom knew that we would be able to interact with bright white students from the north, and thought that these exchanges would offer another opportunity for a balanced learning experience. She didn't want us to think that all white people were the same. Mother was the same way about getting us to try different foods. She used to say, try it first, and then know that you don't like it. Don't reject it without at least discovering your dislikes.

Chaney, Goodman, and Schwerner were murdered because of a white supremacy ideology. On one side, there are those who believe all people should be free and entitled to all of the freedoms allowed first, under God, and then under our constitution. They believe in those values that we fought for, and our founding fathers wrote about. On the other side, we have the self-absorbed established race-based ideology that superimposed one race over the other. This racist ideology is comforted in discriminating based upon skin color, and just a desire to see another as inferior. My Granddaddy would say that there are people in this world, who are so desperate to hold onto white supremacy ideology that they would kill to get that point across.

Freedom Summer brought together both courageous northern white student and southern blacks. Both were operating under dangerous circumstances in the south while committed and guided by a shared value: One Man, One Vote. Both felt that our beloved constitution was experiencing a hiccup back in the 1960's, and something needed to be fixed. Blacks felt that the only people who could correct this flaw unencumbered was another "type of white person": educated ones from the north. We thought that they were sensitive to our plight, and was just being good citizens. We thought of them as the Calvary made up of the brightest and bravest of their kind. Making them the perfect candidates to teach the ignorant uneducated southern whites how to embrace humanity. Northern white student had to depend upon black people to teach them how to survive in a world for the unprivileged, a world up to now, unfamiliar to them. Whites could return home and reclaim those lost privileges that they had to forgo while living in the Jim Crow south. Blacks in the south never had them, and the only way for them to obtain normal privileges was with a struggle, in which they were accustomed. Blacks got the help that they needed to gain privileges that should have been their birthright. The fear, anxiety and day-to-day battles in the Jim Crow south faced by the native blacks and northern white students represented a monumental event never experienced in most of our lifetime. The opportunity for a real educational exchange about racism while trying to correct a flaw; and treat a wound.

I believe that one of the major accomplishments of the Freedom Summer movement is that it did more to forged real relationships between black and white people. Perhaps, this was not the original goal, however, it ended up being the bi-product. These white students were perhaps emblazoned with confidence and thought that their skin color would offer some benefit in opening rigid ideological doors.

Perhaps both were naïve as they fought the good fight: What neither counted on was the Rigid, archaic and hostile resistance of the white supremacy backlash. As with the "settin hen on her warm pre- hatching nest mentality", she will not be disturbed. This White supremacy nest that could never be tempered with, and will be protected by any means necessary. They would kill in order to protect and preserve what they deemed as "their way of life.

What would happen if we had a similar movement like that today? Too many are silent when they see something wrong, many of us are afraid to come forward. Many play the waiting and hoping game that someone else will come forward and take up the baton. If I have to think about the real lesson learned from Freedom Summer, it was that we built real coalitions and relationships that seem sorely missing today.

The ugliness of Freedom Summer took place against the backdrop of such beautiful music: Freedom Songs with Negro spiritual influences, folk music, and who could forget the Sound of Motown. Music was our saving Grace....

DEDICATION

This book is dedicated to the memory of Slain Civil Right Heroes:

James Earl Chaney, Michael Schwerner, and Andrew Goodman. Yes, "You were honorable men who died for an honorable cause. Although you were victims, you did not die in vain. And Yes, there is victory. You are victorious because you believed, and were faithful to the remarkable tenets of Our Founding Fathers who ascribes to:

"We hold these truths to be self evident that all men were created equal, they are endowed by their creator with certain inalienable rights, that among them are life, liberty, and the pursuit of happiness. Yes, there is victory, because you will continue to live through us, and we honor you now and forever.

I am grateful for the encouragement that I received from the family members of the martyrs to finish this book and tell my story.

This book is dedicated to God and My Mother, Ida Bernice Sims, without their comforting spirits and encouragement, this book would not have been written.

ACKNOWLEDGEMENTS:

I owe my deepest gratitude to my Editors at Create Space and, My Book

Designer, David Gilkey. Both of whom have exhibited the patience of Job, God's Faithful Servant.

I am heart fully thankful to my many professional colleagues, friends and family members whose encouragement, guidance and support lead me to greater challenges. I am especially grateful for the friendship and support of Tara V. Young (my muse) and author, Herb Boyd who was always in the wings rooting for me. I am eternally grateful to author, Keith W. Medley, We As Freemen-Plessey v. Ferguson for his support and giving me my first writing assignment in content organization before Katrina devastated his beloved New Orleans.

I am indebted to authors: Phil Dray & Seth Cagin: *We Are Not Afraid.* They gave me support and provided clarity about the role of "the kids" and the underlying strategies that was taking place during the Mississippi Freedom Movement. Their well-developed research about that period was an invaluable resource. I am grateful for their support in giving me the go head to write my story.

I am especially grateful to Mark Levy, Donna Garde, Patti Miller, and Gail Falk for their encouragement and the 1964 Freedom Summer photos. Many family members and friends supported and encouraged me in this project. I owe my deepest gratitude to my baby sister, Marilyn D. Sims whose support alleviated many obstacles. Special thanks to my son, Lyle and his family for their timely support and prayers. I wish to thank my sister Lil who confirmed my life's path when I had doubts. I am thankful for my son, Winston, Jr. and close friends who were waiting patiently in the rooting section. Many thanks to friends Cheryl Smyler and Shirley Cooper for reading my first draft eons ago. I wish to also thank my friend Klyde H. Epps, and Judith Mitchell for their patience and support. *I am very grateful for my friend E.P McKnight for her continued support and in assisting me with book title.*

AUTHOR: BERNICE SIMS

Bernice Sims, LCSW/ACSW, is a veteran of the civil rights movement, having been an active member of NAACP, COFO, and CORE since she was a teenager in the early 1960s. She later left Mississippi to move to New York, where she graduated from Adelphi University and went on to become a social worker.

Sims was elected the first African American female to serve as councilperson on Long Island; she also served on the advisory board for former New York Governor Mario Cuomo. Additionally, Sims has contributed to the art community as a SAG actor, a visual artist, and a writer.

Detour Before Midnight is her personal account of the last few hours she and her family spent with the Mississippi Burning civil rights workers, before they were abducted and murdered by the KKK on June 21, 1964.

Made in the USA
Middletown, DE
16 February 2019